MW00509193

Jérôme Berclaz

Tracking Pedestrians from Multiple Cameras

Computer Vision techniques for multiple
people localization, tracking and behavior
analysis using several cameras

LAP LAMBERT Academic Publishing

Impressum/Imprint (nur für Deutschland/ only for Germany)
Bibliografische Information der Deutschen Nationalbibliothek: Die Deutsche Nationalbibliothek
verzeichnet diese Publikation in der Deutschen Nationalbibliografie; detaillierte bibliografische
Daten sind im Internet über http://dnb.d-nb.de abrufbar.
Alle in diesem Buch genannten Marken und Produktnamen unterliegen warenzeichen-, marken-
oder patentrechtlichem Schutz bzw. sind Warenzeichen oder eingetragene Warenzeichen der
jeweiligen Inhaber. Die Wiedergabe von Marken, Produktnamen, Gebrauchsnamen,
Handelsnamen, Warenbezeichnungen u.s.w. in diesem Werk berechtigt auch ohne besondere
Kennzeichnung nicht zu der Annahme, dass solche Namen im Sinne der Warenzeichen- und
Markenschutzgesetzgebung als frei zu betrachten wären und daher von jedermann benutzt
werden dürften.

Coverbild: www.ingimage.com

Verlag: LAP LAMBERT Academic Publishing AG & Co. KG
Dudweiler Landstr. 99, 66123 Saarbrücken, Deutschland
Telefon +49 681 3720-310, Telefax +49 681 3720-3109
Email: info@lap-publishing.com

Herstellung in Deutschland:
Schaltungsdienst Lange o.H.G., Berlin
Books on Demand GmbH, Norderstedt
Reha GmbH, Saarbrücken
Amazon Distribution GmbH, Leipzig
ISBN: 978-3-8383-6429-2

Imprint (only for USA, GB)
Bibliographic information published by the Deutsche Nationalbibliothek: The Deutsche
Nationalbibliothek lists this publication in the Deutsche Nationalbibliografie; detailed
bibliographic data are available in the Internet at http://dnb.d-nb.de.
Any brand names and product names mentioned in this book are subject to trademark, brand
or patent protection and are trademarks or registered trademarks of their respective holders.
The use of brand names, product names, common names, trade names, product descriptions
etc. even without a particular marking in this works is in no way to be construed to mean that
such names may be regarded as unrestricted in respect of trademark and brand protection
legislation and could thus be used by anyone.

Cover image: www.ingimage.com

Publisher: LAP LAMBERT Academic Publishing AG & Co. KG
Dudweiler Landstr. 99, 66123 Saarbrücken, Germany
Phone +49 681 3720-310, Fax +49 681 3720-3109
Email: info@lap-publishing.com

Printed in the U.S.A.
Printed in the U.K. by (see last page)
ISBN: 978-3-8383-6429-2

Contents

List of Figures

List of Tables

Glossary

A_t^c — ideal random image generated by putting rectangles $\mathscr{A}_k^c$ where $X_t^k = 1$, thus a function of $\mathbf{X}_t$

C — number of cameras

K — number of locations in the ground discretization ($\simeq 1000$)

T — number of time steps

$W \times H$ — image resolution

X^k — Boolean random variable standing for the occupancy of location k on the ground plane

$\mathbf{B}_t$ — binary images generated by the background subtraction $\mathbf{B}_t = (B_t^1, \ldots, B_t^C)$

$\mathbf{I}_t$ — images from all the cameras at time t, $\mathbf{I}_t = (I_t^1, \ldots, I_t^C)$

$\mathbf{X}_t$ — vectors of boolean random variable $(X_t^1, \ldots, X_t^K)$ standing for the occupancy of location k on the ground plane $(X_t^k = 1) \Leftrightarrow (\exists n, L_t^n = k)$

$\mathscr{A}_k^c$ — the image composed of 1s inside a rectangle standing for the silhouette of an individual at location k seen from camera c, and 0s elsewhere

POM Detector

ε_k — the prior probability of presence at location k, $P(X^k = 1)$

λ_k — is $\log \frac{1-\varepsilon_k}{\varepsilon_k}$, the log-ratio of the prior probability

$\overline{A}_{k,\xi}^c$ — compact notation for the average synthetic image $E_Q(A^c \mid X^k = \xi)$, see Figure 3.2

Ψ — a pseudo-distance between images

E_Q — Expectation under $\mathbf{X} \sim Q$, $E_Q(x) = \int x Q(x) dx$.

$I \oplus J$ — disjunction of images, $\forall (x,y)$, $(I \oplus J)(x,y) = 1 - (1 - I(x,y))(1 - J(x,y))$

$I \otimes J$ — intersection of images, $\forall (x,y)$, $(I \otimes J)(x,y) = I(x,y)J(x,y)$

Q — the product law used to approximate, for a fixed t, the real posterior distribution $P(\cdot \mid \mathbf{B}_t)$

q_k — the marginal probability of Q, that is $Q(X_k = 1)$

Classification-Based Detector

$\delta^c(i,j)$ — horizontal distance between the centers of $\mathscr{I}_i^c$ and $\mathscr{I}_j^c$ on camera view c

$\mathbf{T}$ — vector of all trees' ansers T_k^c

E_R — expectation under $\mathbf{X} \sim R$. $E_R(x) = \int x R(x) dx$.

n_k^c — neighborhood of k on camera c, $\left\{ j \neq k, \mathscr{I}_j^c \cap \mathscr{I}_k^c \neq \emptyset \right\}$

R — the product law with the same marginals as the real posterior distribution $P(\cdot \mid \mathbf{T})$. $R(\mathbf{X}) = \prod_{k=1}^K R(X^k)$

T_k^c — sum of the responses of the binary decision trees at ground location k in camera view c, thus an integer value in $\{0, \ldots, N_T\}$ where N_T is the number of decision trees

$\mathscr{I}_k^c$ — rectangular human size sub-window cropped from camera view c at ground location k

r_k — the marginal probability of R, i.e. $R(X^k = 1)$

Dynamic-Programming tracker

$\mathbf{L}^n$ — trajectory of individual n, $\mathbf{L}^n = (L_1^n, \ldots, L_T^n)$

$\mathbf{L}_t$ — vector of people locations on the ground plane or in the hidden location $\mathbf{L}_t = (L_t^1, \ldots, L_t^{N^*})$. Each of these random variables takes values into $\{1, \ldots, K, \mathscr{H}\}$, where $\mathscr{H}$ is the hidden place

μ_n^c — color distribution of individual n from camera c

N^* — virtual number of people, including the non-visible ones

S_t — texture information

Linear-Programming tracker

$\mathfrak{F}$ — set of occupancy maps physically possible

$\mathfrak{H}$ — set of flows physically possible, i.e. satisfying the constraints of Eqs. 4.26, 4.27, 4.28, and 4.35

$e_{i,j}^t$ — directed edge from location i at time t to location j at time $t+1$

$f_{i,j}^t$	estimated number of objects moving from location i at time t to location j at time $t+1$
M_i^t	random variable standing for the true number of objects at location i at time t
m_i^t	estimated number of objects at location i at time t
$\mathcal{N}(k)$	$\subset \{1,\ldots,K\}$ neighborhood of location k

Behavior Models

κ	Gaussian kernel
$\mathbf{f}_u$	trajectory fragment
$\mathbf{F}_u^k$	r.v. standing for the true location of the individual of fragment u at step k
$\mathbf{f}_u^k$	k-th point of the trajectory fragment
$\mu_{q,m}$	probability distribution of control point q of map m over the behavioral maps
$f_{q,m}$	probability distribution of control point q of map m over the grid locations
L_t	random process standing for the position in the grid of an individual, and taking values in $\{1,\ldots,K\}$
M	number of behavioral maps

M_t	random process standing for the behavioral map that a person is currently following, taking values in $\{1,\ldots,M\}$
M_u^k	r.v. standing for the true map followed by the individual of fragment u at step k
Q	Number of control points

Acronyms

CCTV	Closed-Circuit Television
E-M	Expectation-Maximization algorithm
HMM	Hidden Markov Model
JPDAF	Joint Probability Data Assocation Filter
MCMC	Markov Chain Monte Carlo
MHT	Multiple Hypothesis Tracking
MODA	Multiple Object Detection Accuracy
MODP	Multiple Object Detection Precision
MOTA	Multiple Object Tracking Accuracy
MOTP	Multiple Object Tracking Precision
PCA	Principal Component Analysis
POM	Probabilistic Occupancy Map

Chapter 1

Introduction

Recent years have witnessed rapid advances in the field of Computer Vision. On the one hand, the steady growth in available computational power has made possible the real-time implementation of complex algorithms that were too resource-consuming to be usable a decade ago. On the other hand, miniaturization and low production costs of circuitry - and particularly vision sensors, such as CCD or CMOS - have contributed to the widespread inclusion of cameras in electronic devices. Cameras have become so ubiquitous today that there are very few cell phones, portable media players, PDA or laptops that do not include at least one. Furthermore, we now notably find embedded cameras in cars, elevators, airplanes or houses.

Following the same tendency, public security cameras have seen their number dramatically increasing in urban environments. Besides owing to the technology advances, this phenomenon is also driven by a growing sense of insecurity among the population along with some highly publicized tragic events. The trend started with the usage of cameras for road monitoring - the number of cameras dedicated to traffic law enforcement in the United Kingdom has increased from 300,000 in 1996 to over 2 million in 2004 [6] - and is now proceeding with general crime prevention inside cities. According to [6], an estimated 4.2 million[1] Closed-circuit television (CCTV) cameras were active in 2006 in the UK, which amounts to almost one for every 14 people. And this phenomenon concerns almost all major western cities: In 2002, between 7,000 and 12,000 cameras were installed in Berlin [122] in retail shops only, a total of 25,000 cameras were estimated in Oslo [129], around 60,000 were officially censused in France [69], and a huge 500,000 in London [84]. These cameras are primarily located in potentially crowded areas, such as airports, stations, shopping malls, stadiums or touristic attractions.

However, among all these cameras, only a small fraction is actively monitored. Although some very specific monitoring tasks can be performed by an automated system, such as traffic speeding reporting, the state-of-the-art is not yet advanced enough for the highly complex task of anomaly detection in an urban environment.

---

[1]Note that this number includes public and privately owned surveillance cameras.

Therefore, most of today's surveillance systems are intrinsically passive devices, used mostly for forensic crime investigation and for their potentially preventive effect, although the incidence of surveillance cameras on the crime rate is still debated [128].

In this context, there is a huge research effort aimed at increasing the level of automation and making more effective use of all these cameras by reducing the workload of human operators. The ultimate goal is to have an intelligent system that can monitor in real-time a typical urban center crowded with people and cars, detect and identify any type of potential problems, accidents or threats, and report them automatically to a competent authority. Implementing such a system is very difficult and poses a number of challenges:

- Video sequences, especially outdoor ones, can be of very bad quality. Current sensors have a limited dynamic range and lighting changes, weather effects, and dust can corrupt the images and make them difficult to interpret.

- Identifying, segmenting and localizing pedestrians, cars, and other objects of interest from images is a very complex task, which is still unsolved in its generic form. Those targets can have a wide range of different appearances, are deformable, and often occlude each other. Urban environments are frequently cluttered with obstacles that may occlude, reflect, have a similar appearance or project shadows on the target objects.

- Tracking multiple targets, especially pedestrians, is difficult because they often exhibit complex motions and interact with each other. People frequently move in groups, which eventually split or re-merge with other groups.

- Detecting abnormal situations is challenging, because the variety of different behaviors that naturally occur in any given environment makes the distinction between "normal" and unusual events difficult.

Many researchers have tackled the automated surveillance problem, although most of them concentrate on one specific subtopic: some address only low-level detection of objects, while others try to analyze people behavior by assuming access to perfect trajectory information. Historically, the first approaches have attempted to track people from a single camera [47, 23, 46]. Among them, many rely on blobs from background subtraction as an initial input [48, 22]. They typically combine shape analysis and tracking to locate people, while maintaining appearance models in order to follow them even in the presence of occlusions. More sophisticated approaches also take color into account. A standard way is to combine multiple image cues with MCMC [144] or particle filtering [44, 94, 111] for tracking.

Despite their effectiveness in sparse crowds, monocular approaches have limited capabilities to deal with denser situations, because time consistency alone is not enough to cope with a large number of occlusions. In this context, the use of multiple cameras becomes necessary. Not only is this technique more effective at handling occlusions, but it allows to compute precise 3-D localization of people and can enlarge the monitored field of view. In multi-view, background subtraction is also often a starting point [96, 68, 64]. Approaches fuse the blobs from different views using a visual hull [136], 2-D visual angles [96], or homographic constraints [36, 65]. The resulting ground detections are then typically tracked with particle filters [96], graph cuts [64, 65], or dual-stage frameworks performing one-to-one correspondences followed by a split and merge analysis [36].

Among both monocular and multi-view approaches, some address tracking as a recursive detection problem using methods such as Kalman filtering [85, 14], particle filtering [57, 111], or mean-shift [23]. To overcome their tendency to drift when difficult conditions arise, researchers have attempted to look at a longer time period by incorporating Joint Probabilistic Data Association Filters [61] or Multiple Hypothesis Tracking [46]. However, the search space of these methods grows exponentially with the number of frames. A more recent research trend thus tries to address the problem by decoupling detection from tracking. A detector is applied at each time step independently and a data association method links the detections together, producing more robust results. Various methods have been tried for data association, such as graph cuts [64], dynamic programming [10], linear programming [59], min-cost flow [140], or variants of AdaBoost to automatically learn the best associations [76].

Approaches specifically targeted at learning behavior models from pedestrian data often rely on trajectories clustering [101, 90, 3, 98] or vector quantization [60, 113]. Some build their behavior model directly in the image view [113, 90], while others project the trajectories on the ground plane first [101, 3]. More complex approaches include [9], which applies an E-M algorithm to cluster trajectories recorded with laser-range finders. From this data, they derive an HMM to predict future position of the people. Similarly, [2] characterizes crowd behavior by observing the crowd optical flow and uses unsupervised feature extraction to encode normal crowd behavior. PCA is applied to extract motion models, which are combined through an HMM.

In this work, we propose a bottom-up approach for pedestrian behavior analysis from multiple cameras that avoids the pitfalls encountered by the methods presented above. Notably, we separate our system into 3 modules that work almost independently, allowing them to easily recover from errors.

Detection We first build a robust people detector from multiple views, which works on a frame-by-frame basis and merges information from different cameras to produce an accurate localization on the ground plane. The method uses a sophisticated generative model to naturally handle occlusions. Not requiring time-consistency makes our method very robust to occasional failure, and avoids drift problems commonly faced by methods that combine detection and tracking.

Tracking In a second step, we design a multi-object linking method to connect detections produced by our first module. It relies on global optimization to extract complex trajectories of interacting people over a large number of frames, while avoiding local minima caused by occasional miss-detections. The generality of the approach makes it also well suited for other applications than pedestrian tracking.

Behavior analysis Finally, we introduce a novel model to represent the most typical motion patterns that people follow in a specific environment. Our model encodes different types of observed behavior, and is learnt by collecting data from our detector over an extended period of time. The method is made robust by only requiring time independent detections as input instead of full trajectories. The resulting behavior model can be used in conjunction with our people tracker, to classify the extracted trajectories as *normal* or *abnormal*. Furthermore, this model can be incorporated into a tracker to improve the quality of trajectories.

Several potential applications exist for the system presented in this book. Surveillance is the obvious one. Although capturing trajectories is not informative enough to fully understand complex situations involving humans, it is sufficient to spot unusual events in environments where the main human motions are simple, such as a passageway or corridor.

Furthermore, surveillance is not the only area that can benefit from a system such as ours. Behavior analysis for customer market research in shops is growing in importance. The knowledge of how people navigate and how their paths correlate with sales is of great value for shop owners, who are constantly trying to increase the attractivity of their retail location. In this context, producing metrically accurate trajectories and extracting significant motion patterns from them is extremely useful.

Another example comes from team sports, such as soccer or basketball. Players intensively interact in very complex patterns over almost two hours. A precise analysis of the their actions during the match is very important for coaches to evaluate the performance of their team and of individual players. It could also be used to analyze the opposing team's tactics. Doing this by watching hours of video is tedious and would greatly benefit from automation, especially if the system were accurate enough to catch subtle behaviors.

To be readily applicable to the aforementioned activities, a tracking system must be robust, that is follow people accurately with a minimum amount of identity switches, miss-detections and false positives, even in suboptimal conditions. Precision is also an essential characteristic for gathering significant statistical data about people motion. Equally important, it needs to be capable of recovering from occasional tracking mistakes, in order to run over a long period of time. The realization of such a system is the objective of this work, which we define more precisely in the rest of this chapter.

1.1 Goals

The goal of this work is first to *detect* and *track* an *a priori* unknown number of people using multiple cameras. We then want to *infer* a behavior model for a given environment by passively monitoring the scene. More specifically, we aim at

- robustly detecting multiple people in spite of occlusions, which are inevitable when the cameras are not looking strictly down;

- precisely locating these people in world coordinates;

- reliably linking detections into trajectories, despite potential miss-detections and false positives;

- learning a behavior model in places where people do indeed tend to follow standard patterns, and using it to classify detected trajectories;

- relying on standard off-the-shelf video equipment only;

- designing fast algorithms - for detection and tracking - that could be run in real-time on standard computers.

Combining these requirements results in a robust framework that can be applied to typical surveillance environments, in which light is not controlled and camera positioning is constrained. In the following section, we outline our research efforts towards attaining these specifications.

1.2 Overview of our Approach

As mentioned earlier, we advocate an approach in which detection and tracking are decoupled. Detection is performed on a frame-by-frame basis, which makes it robust to failures: Because we do not enforce temporal consistency, a failure at time t does not influence the result at time $t + 1$. Moreover, this approach can handle streams of any frame rate, including slow ones that imply large motions between frames. We briefly outline the components of our system below.

1.2.1   People Detection

To detect people, we discretize the ground plane into a grid of cells. We start by performing background subtraction independently on every available view. We then approximate the marginal conditional probabilities of occupancy of the ground plane given the background subtraction images from all views acquired at the same time. This approximation is obtained by minimizing the Kullback-Leibler divergence between a product law and the true posterior under a generative model. We show that this is equivalent to computing marginal probabilities of occupancy so that, under the product law, the images obtained by putting rectangles of human sizes at occupied locations are likely to be similar to the images actually produced by the background subtraction. By estimating occupancy directly in the ground plane, we produce probabilistic occupancy maps that indicate precisely where people are most likely to be. Moreover, this approach fuses multiple camera views in a manner that naturally takes occlusions into account.

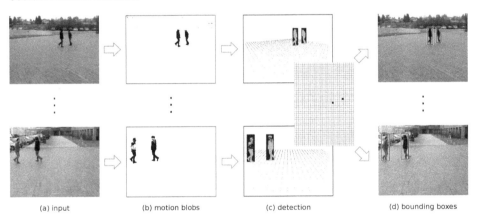

(a) input   (b) motion blobs   (c) detection   (d) bounding boxes

Figure 1.1: An overview of our approach for people detection: original images (a) are processed individually by background subtraction yielding binary images (b). These are merged using a generative model of the background subtraction, which estimates ground occupancy (c). Finally, the detection in images is performed by projecting the bounding boxes (d) corresponding to the occupied locations of the ground.

We also experiment with an alternate approach that replaces the background subtraction by a classifier trained at recognizing pedestrians in individual images. For each image, the classifier is applied to sub-images corresponding to every location of the ground plane grid. This generates a map of classifier answers per camera view, which are later merged using a generative model of the classifier response. By applying classifiers instead of background subtraction, this method is able to concentrate on pedestrians, while ignoring other types of object motion. Despite its theoretical interest, this alternate approach does not produce results that match the quality of those from our first method, and is too resource-consuming to be applied in practice.

1.2.2 People Tracking

We experimented with two separate approaches to recovering trajectories from detections, both of which rely on global optimization applied to probabilistic occupancy maps generated by our people detector. The global optimization scheme is generally more robust than the recursive update of estimates from frame to frame, which may fail if difficult conditions persist over several consecutive frames. By contrast, our algorithms handle such situations, since we compute the global optima of scores summed over many frames.

We first propose a multiple-people tracking method based on Dynamic Programming. Video sequences are processed by batches of 100 frames, and the most likely trajectory is computed for each individual. To avoid the complexity of the joint optimization, we extract individual trajectories independently. In theory, this approach could lead to undesirable local minima, for example, by connecting the trajectories of two separate people. To reduce the chances of this, we process individual trajectories in an order that depends on a reliability score, so that the most reliable ones are computed first, thereby reducing the potential for confusion when processing the remaining ones. The optimization is performed on the ground occupancy probabilities provided by the people detector, combined with a color-histogram-based appearance model and a simple isotropic motion model.

Figure 1.2: An example of tracking results based on Linear Programming on a relatively crowded sequence. Each row shows a different camera view out of the 4 originally available. Each column shows a different time frame. Two consecutive columns are separated by 20 frames. Note the large number of occlusions due to the camera placement.

We then introduce a second approach to multiple people tracking that performs joint trajectory optimization over a batch of frames using Linear Programming. We formulate the linking step as a constrained flow optimization, which results in a convex problem that can be solved using Linear Programming techniques. The complexity of the resulting Linear Program is very high, but we show that, due to its particular structure, our problem can be solved very efficiently using the k-shortest paths algorithm [117]. This optimized algorithm performs up to 1,000 times faster than a generic Linear Programming solver, while producing the exact same result.

1.2.3 Behavior Analysis

In the last part of this document, we introduce models that can both describe how people move on a location of interest's ground plane, such as a cafeteria, a corridor, or a train station, and be learned from ground occupancy maps provided by a people detector. We represent specific behaviors by a set of *behavioral maps* that encode, for each ground plane location, the probability of moving in a particular direction. We then associate to people being tracked a probability of acting according to an individual map and to switch from one to the other based on their location. The maps and model parameters are learned by Expectation-Maximization in a completely unsupervised fashion. At run-time, they are used for efficient detection of abnormal behavior by computing the probability of retrieved trajectories under the estimated model. Also, we show that those maps are well suited to replace the simple isotropic motion model used by our Dynamic Programming-based tracker, with a more sophisticated one adapted to a specific environment.

1.3 Outline

The remainder of this document is structured as follows: In Chapter 2, we introduce the framework on which our system is built. We also briefly expose some of the methods used by our system, but that were not precisely the focus of this work, such as camera calibration or background subtraction. In Chapter 3, we explain our main method for people detection and introduce an alternate one based on classification. In Chapter 4, we propose and evaluate two separate tracking methods relying on global optimization. In Chapter 5, we develop an approach to automatically learn behavioral maps by monitoring a scene with the detector of Chapter 3. Related work about people detection, tracking and behavior analysis will be discussed separately at the beginning of each corresponding chapter. Finally, after some perspectives for future work, we conclude in Chapter 6.

Chapter 2

Framework

Despite the tremendous progress of Computer Vision during the last four decades, the general vision problem is far from being solved. As a consequence, current vision applications need to be quite heavily constrained to produce meaningful results. People detection and tracking is no exception. In particular, it is still beyond the current state-of-the-art to expect a very general tracker, which would be able to follow people accurately in any situation, regardless of the environment, light, people density and activity, etc.

This chapter introduces the framework on which we build our approach to pedestrian detection, tracking, and behavior analysis. We explain our motivations for the design choices and trade-offs underlying our application. We also outline some of the auxiliary methods used by our system, such as camera calibration or background subtraction. They do not constitute the focus of our work but are required to make the system work. Finally, we present the test data and the metrics we use to evaluate the performance of our algorithms.

2.1 Design Choices

The goal of this work is to build a vision-based pedestrian tracking system that is both robust and precise enough to allow meaningful people behavior analysis based on the retrieved trajectories. More precisely, we want to design our system with the following characteristics:

- it has to be able to follow an *a priori* unknown and potentially varying number of people;

- it must supply accurate localization in world coordinates - as opposed to an imprecise image detection - allowing behavior analysis based on trajectories;

- it only requires off-the-shelf video equipment, as opposed to cutting edge technology like high resolution video, infrared images or stereo cameras;

9

- it is adaptable to non-optimal camera placement and various number of cameras, in order to be usable in the widest possible range of environments.

2.1.1 Multiple Cameras

To fulfill these requirements, we made a number of design choices, the most important of which was the decision to rely on a multi-camera system. Multiple people moving tend to occlude each other, which generates ambiguity when observed by a single camera. When the number of people is small, researchers usually address this issue by relying on time consistency. However, when the people density increases, the large amount of occlusions produced renders any monocular tracking task very difficult. These ambiguities may be eliminated by images taken from another viewpoint. Although this issue can also be partly addressed by using a single top mounted camera that may reduce the amount of occlusion, this solution is not without flaws. An indoor top camera can be close to useless if the ceiling is not high enough. This limitation can be overcome with the help of a Fisheye lens, however this type of lenses also heavily distorts the resulting image and makes its treatment difficult. Additionally, when placed outdoors, a top camera involves a significantly more complex setup than a regular one.

Since the useful field of view of any type of camera is limited, using multiple cameras is also a way to expand the surveillance area. Furthermore, it provides more accurate localizations than a single camera setup.

2.1.2 Camera Placement

In most indoor environments monitored by video, camera placement is heavily constrained due to the low ceiling height. This creates a challenge not only because cameras looking obliquely are more prone to occlusions but also because the 3-D localization is less precise when the camera is close to the ground.

Nevertheless, we decided to design our system specifically for this suboptimal camera placement where cameras are located just slightly higher than a person's head, because that type of environment is one of the most commonly encountered in video surveillance situations. That said, our approach is sufficiently flexible to adapt to other types of camera placement.

Since we use the redundant information provided by several cameras at different points of view, the fields of view overlap needs to be maximized, and the viewpoints as diverse as possible for optimal results. Extensive studies [88] have been devoted to camera placement in multi-camera systems, but in our case, the system performance is not very sensitive to it.

Our system can handle any number of cameras. For best results though, more than one camera are needed. As a rule of thumb, the higher the people density, the more cameras are necessary to overcome the occlusion ambiguity. Note that our approach is totally scalable and can even work monocularly, when there are relatively few occlusions

2.1.3 Constraints

To bound the complexity of our task, a certain number of assumptions have been made. First of all, in this work, we assume that the ground plane on which people evolve is flat. This assumption considerably simplifies our calibration procedure, as will be shown in §2.4. This is however not to say that our system could not work on uneven grounds. Provided with an elevation model of the ground, our framework extends very well to non-flat ground surfaces. Nonetheless, acquiring an elevation model of the ground is in itself a time consuming task on which we did not want to focus this work.

Another implicit assumption is that pedestrians are the only moving objects in our scenes. This constraint reduces the generality of the system in cases where people interact with other moving objects, such as cars. Therefore a city center cluttered with cars or an airport apron would not be reliably monitored by our system in its current state.

Finally, we also assume that the people we track are pedestrians, which is to say that they are always in upright position, whether they stand, walk or run. Although this constraint slightly limits the generality of our system, moving pedestrians are by far the most interesting target for people tracking systems. Additionally, we will see in Chapter 3.2.6 that our system is quite tolerant and robust to several human activities that depart significantly from walking, such as basketball playing.

2.2 Occupancy Map

One of the challenges of multiple views is the necessary fusion of the information provided by individual sensors. This has been usually addressed by projecting detections from individual views into a common 3-D reference, and using various geometry-based heuristics to cluster the detections belonging to the same object. For example, [30] uses a Bayesian network to fuse 2-D state vectors acquired from various image sequences to obtain a 3-D state vector. [120] relies on nearest neighbor Kalman filter for fusing observations into a single estimate. [133] uses a two-level hierarchy of Kalman filters for trajectory tracking and data fusion from multiple cameras. In this work, we propose two different approaches to tackle data fusion from multiple views. Both have in common the use of an occupancy grid to represent the ground plane. Instead of relying on continuous geometric coordinates to locate the detected objects in a common reference plane, we discretize the ground plane into a finite number of cells, and estimate their occupancy individually. An occupancy grid represents a powerful tool for data fusion from multiple sensors [114], and it extends very well to tracking and behavior analysis, without sacrificing the localization precision.

The concept of occupancy grid was first introduced by [32], and has been extensively used since then in the robotic navigation literature [107, 121]. An occupancy grid consists of a multi-dimensional random field that maintains stochastic estimate of the occupancy state of the cells in a spatial lattice. Although mostly used as a two-dimensional structure, it has been also extended to 3-D [40] and used for reconstructing 3-D models from different views.

In our framework, a two dimensional probabilistic occupancy map with K cells is used to represent the ground plane occupancy. The individual cells are typically squares of 20×20 cm to 30×30 cm, which represents slightly less than the space occupied by a standing pedestrian. The usual size of the grids we deal with is of the order of $K \simeq 1,000$ cells, and varies with respect to the tracking area dimension. Concrete examples are given in §2.7.

Throughout this work, we always deal with plain rectangular grids, because they are very convenient to derive from a camera calibration, and easy to deal with in a computer program. However, nothing stops us from using arbitrary-shaped grids as well as non-planar ones, if those fit better the tracking environment. Besides, our approach is also compatible with non regular grids, such as the one proposed in [1].

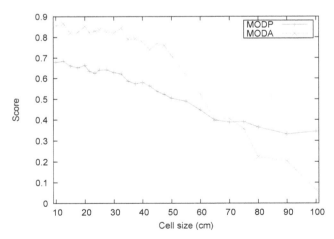

Figure 2.1: Determining optimal grid resolution. Detection accuracy (MODA) and precision (MODP) are plotted as a function of the cell size. We see that, although precision decreases almost linearly with cell size, accuracy starts dropping for sizes larger than 35 cm.

The grid resolution cannot be chosen arbitrarily, because inappropriate values might seriously affect the performance of the people detector. Obviously, coarse resolutions should be avoided, because we do not want more than one person to fit simultaneously into a single grid cell. If this was possible, our detector would lose discrimination power when people are close to each other. Moreover, it is desirable that, wherever a person is standing, there is a grid cell that approximates its position well enough. To quantify the importance of the grid resolution, we show in Fig. 2.1 the performance variation of the people detector of Chapter 3.2 for different cell sizes. The graph was obtained by running people detection on a video sequence and evaluating the result against a manually labelled ground truth with standard detection metrics. The exact metrics definition is given in §2.6, but for this example it is suffi-cient to know that the precision metric (MODP) gauges the alignment of the detec-tions with respect to the reference, and the accuracy metric (MODA) roughly counts the false positives and negatives. As expected, we see that the precision (MODP) decreases linearly as the cell size grows larger. By contrast the accuracy (MODA) is stable up to 35 cm, and then starts decreasing. Beyond this critical value, the dis-cretization is no longer fine enough to correctly approximate all possible positions of the ground plane. For this reason, in our experiments, we always use cell sizes of 30 cm or less.

2.3 Modeling People

At the heart of the people detector of Chapter 3.2 is a generative model for back-ground subtraction images. We motivate here the choice of the simple rectangular shapes we adopt for human silhouettes approximation in the model.

A human body is a challenging object to model, because it is both highly artic-ulated and deformable. As suggested by the example set of silhouettes in Fig. 2.2, pedestrian silhouettes can take very different shapes. They can be even more het-erogeneous when people perform activities different from walking, such as running or playing sports . Therefore, no particular fixed shape can faithfully capture the wide range of potential silhouettes generated by pedestrians, and one has to rely on complex articulated models.

Figure 2.2: Some examples of typical pedestrian silhouettes.

Instead, we observe that usual pedestrian silhouettes share a common size and as-pect ratio. More generally, pedestrians occupy a portion of space that can be roughly approximated by a cylinder of 50 cm diameter and 175 cm height, as illustrated by

Figure 2.3: This figure illustrates how the space occupied by pedestrians can reasonably well be approximated with cylinders of 50 cm diameter and 1.75 meter high. The right image shows that the cylinders projection in the image plane is close enough to vertical rectangles, when the camera is located sufficiently low relatively to the ground.

Fig. 2.3. Furthermore, when observed by a camera positioned around 2 m above the ground, with a standard lens, the cylinders project into the camera images as slightly rounded rectangles, which can be reasonably approximated by vertical rectangles aligned to the image coordinate system.

Based on this reasoning, we model the foreground blobs produced by a person on a binary background subtraction image with a rectangle of aspect ratio 2:7. Examples are illustrated by Fig. 2.4. The choice of a rectangle shape for foreground silhouette approximation is further motivated by efficiency constraints of the people detection algorithm: In Chapter 3, we show that this shape allows us to significantly speed up some computation by relying on integral images [126]. Other research work have proposed the use of more sophisticated shape models for human foreground blobs. For example, [57] uses the 2-D projection of a cylinder with varying diameter, while [1] suggests the use of a semi-elliptical shape for the same purpose. Some approaches rely on 3-D shapes, such as [96], which proposes cylinders with an elliptical base or [143], which uses ellipsoids as a 3-D human shape model. A summary of the most common 2-D representations for human silhouettes is depicted by Fig. 2.5.

Note that our model for silhouettes has been specifically conceived for the particular setup in which cameras are oriented horizontally and located at about the same height as people heads. As one significantly departs from this original setup, for example by placing the cameras very high, the model becomes progressively no longer adapted. However, by redefining the silhouette model, the generative model of Chapter 3.2.2 can be easily adapted to a wide range of environments, such as, for example, the tracking of table tennis balls that we illustrate in Chapter 4.3.7 or tracking pedestrians from a ceiling mounted Fisheye camera.

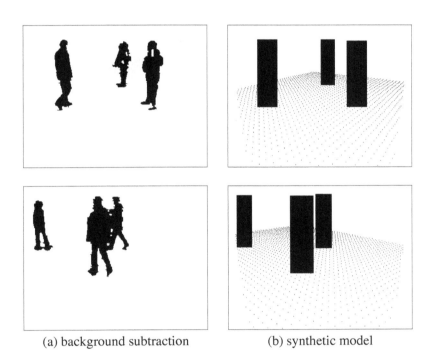

(a) background subtraction (b) synthetic model

Figure 2.4: Background subtraction images with human silhouettes (a), with their corresponding synthetic model (b). Note that the dots are not part of the synthetic model, but are simply printed to show the extent of the ground plane grid.

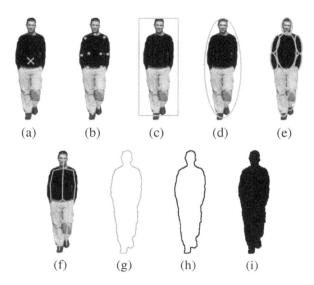

Figure 2.5: Different types of people representation found in the literature: (a) centroid, (b) multiple points, (c) bounding box, (d) ellipse, (e) multiple ellipses, (f) skeleton, (g) control points, (h) contour and (i) silhouette.

2.4 Camera Calibration

Multi-view-based tracking draws its main strength from the additional information provided by different view points, which can overcome occlusion. But this extra knowledge can only be fully exploited if the connection between image measurements and scene measurements is known. In every multi-view approach, detections in individual views eventually need to be related and merged.

This correspondence problem is usually dealt with by computing the cameras calibration, which consists, for every camera, in estimating its *intrinsic parameters* - focal length, principal point and radial distortion, among others - and *extrinsic parameters*, that is, its position and orientation in space. Over the years, several different camera calibration methods [18, 124, 142] have been developed. Their computation typically requires the definition of correspondences between scene and image measurements. A technique called *autocalibration* [83, 123, 103] allows to trade extensive scene knowledge for knowledge of camera motion. Once estimated, the camera calibration parameters give a precise understanding of the image formation mechanism. A complete discussion of the camera calibration problem extends well beyond the scope of this work, and we refer the interested reader to [49], which covers extensively the multiple aspects of the subject.

In our case, camera calibration is specifically needed to relate people silhouettes in the images to their corresponding position on the ground plane. Reciprocally, for every position of the ground plane, we need to estimate the approximate bounding box in the image view of a pedestrian standing there. This is a well constrained problem, and although it can be solved using standard calibration, we will see that it is sufficient to use a simpler homography-based method, which is more convenient to compute. The simplified method is generally less precise though, and does not take radial distortion into account. Thus, we still use standard calibration methods in larger scenes, for which precision is critical. In the remainder of this section, we first describe our method using homographies, which we dub *homography-based calibration* although it is not strictly speaking a calibration. We then give a brief overview of the Tsai [124] calibration method, which we also used as part of this work.

2.4.1 Homography-Based Calibration

In order to establish the simple rectangular projections needed by our generative model, a full camera calibration is not absolutely necessary. The homography-based camera calibration is a simplified calibration procedure that is specifically tailored for our pedestrian tracking model. Its main advantage stems from the simplicity of the procedure, compared to standard calibration techniques that require numerous real-world measurements.

At the origin of the method are two important assumptions:

1. People are walking on a perfectly flat ground plane;

2. Cameras do not present any type of distortion.

The first assumption is satisfied in many people tracking environments, especially indoor ones, and is a good enough approximation in many others. The second assumption is reasonable when using standard lens types - i.e. not Fisheye - with a moderate focal length - i.e. not smaller than 35 mm on a 35 mm full-frame camera.

This model is based on the idea that people evolving on the ground plane are in fact located between two parallel planes: the ground plane on which they walk and the plane placed approximately 1.75 m above the ground plane, which we refer to as *head plane*. Those two parallel planes are illustrated in Figure 2.6. Contrary to usual calibration methods, the homography-based calibration does not need to estimate all camera parameters. Instead, we just compute the two homographies per camera view that map a top view of the ground plane into the ground plane and respectively the head plane in the camera view.

The two necessary homographies per camera view can be easily computed using the *Direct Linear Transformation* algorithm [49]. The procedure consists in specifying at least 4 point correspondences between the top and the camera views. A

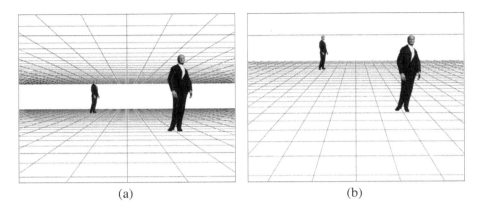

(a)   (b)

Figure 2.6: People evolving on a flat ground are located between two planes: the ground plane and the head plane (a). When the camera is placed at the same height as the head plane (b), the head plane appears as a single line in the camera view.

degenerate case occurs when the camera is placed at the exact same height as the head plane. In this situation, all points from the head plane are projected into a single line in the camera view, as shown by Fig. 2.6(b), and the homography is ill-defined. When this happens, we do not attempt to compute the homography, but instead record the height of the projected line in the image. This is enough to generate the synthetic views by projecting the appropriate rectangles into the image.

At this point, the homography-based method still needs real-world measurements to define correspondences with the image views. To address this limitation and make the calibration procedure more convenient, we have implemented a method inspired by [70]. This technique uses the motion segmentation of a person walking in front of the cameras to estimate points in both the ground and the head planes. It then uses these point correspondences to derive the two homographies. The method can be made robust to background subtraction imprecision by using RANSAC [38]. The method we developed [45] adapts this solution to our problem, for which we need not only homographies between camera views but also homographies between top and camera views.

2.4.2   Tsai Calibration Model

When at least one of the assumptions of the homography-based calibration cannot be fulfilled, we use the more complete Tsai calibration model, originally described by Roger Tsai in [124]. This method fully estimates both intrinsic and extrinsic camera parameters, as well as the first order coefficient of radial distortion. To retrieve accurate parameters, the method requires about 20-30 correspondences between 3-D

| (a) Reference frame | (b) Input frame | (c) Motion segmentation |

Figure 2.7: Typical example of background subtraction: A reference frame (a) is used as background model, and an input image (b) is compared to it, generating a corresponding binary motion segmentation (c), in which moving parts are depicted in black. This particular background subtraction example was made with mixtures of Gaussians.

points in world coordinate and their image projection counterparts.

Since the Tsai model recovers the complete calibration parameters, one can project any 3-D point in the camera images, making this method well suited for non-flat ground. Also, its ability to retrieve radial distortion is helpful when dealing with wide angle lenses. In our work, we rely on the Tsai model instead of the simpler homography-based one when handling large areas. For locations far from the camera, a small error due to radial distortion gets amplified and leads to misalignments between views.

2.5 Background Subtraction

Background Subtraction [100], also commonly referred to as *Change Detection* or *Motion Segmentation*, is a simple yet powerful technique for detecting motion from a video stream filmed by a static camera. In its most basic form, it simply consists in comparing every new image from the stream to a reference model, and labeling as *motion* all the pixels that depart significantly from the model. Background subtraction thus usually produces binary images, in which static parts are segmented from dynamic ones. Probabilistic images, where every pixel is assigned a probability to belong to the background are also sometimes generated. Figure 2.7 displays an example of background subtraction using mixtures of Gaussians.

An ideal background subtraction algorithm should react to moving objects only. However, by only relying on pixel intensities to separate foreground from background, most techniques are subject to potential confusion by a number of elements. First and most obvious, if a moving object has the same appearance as the background, it might go undetected. Moreover, light changes, such as reflections, shadows, variation in light intensity, etc. might be wrongly interpreted as motion. Small background motion, such as tree foliage should be ignored altogether, and stationary

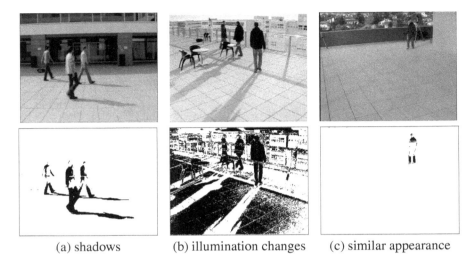

| (a) shadows | (b) illumination changes | (c) similar appearance |

Figure 2.8: Three typical background subtraction failure cases: (a) shadows, (b) rapid illumination changes and (c) foreground objects with similar appearance to the background.

objects - such as a car that was just parked - must at some point be integrated into the background model. Typical background subtraction limitations are depicted by Fig. 2.8.

To cope with some of the challenges mentioned above and go beyond the limitations of the original method, several improvements were devised. For instance, [112] describes every pixel of the background with a mixture of Gaussians. In so doing, this approach is able to model slightly moving backgrounds, such as trees or waves. [33] bases its model on Kernel Density Estimation to achieve the same effect. [95, 104] develop a background subtraction method called *eigenbackgrounds*. As opposed to the approaches mentioned above, which model single pixel locations independently, this technique is capable of learning spatial correlation from different reference images of the background using eigenvalue decomposition. Such a model is thus particularly suited to deal with global illumination changes that affect large parts of the image.

More recently, [73] took advantage of the redundant information provided by a multi-view system to identify and remove the shadows projected on the ground from background subtraction images. Instead of the traditional statistical background model, [102] uses a statistical illumination model, in order to handle sudden illumination changes.

Even though some elements developed in this work rely on background subtraction, this topic is not in itself our main focus. Therefore, we do not expand further on this subject and refer the interested reader to the articles cited above.

Throughout this work, we used different background subtraction implementations, the choice of which depended on their performance in various environments. Most of the results presented in this work have been processed with our own implementation of the eigenbackground [95] algorithm. On some particular sequences, we relied on the method developed in [102] or an in-house implementation using mixtures of Gaussians. In our system, the background subtraction is thus considered as a black box, which produces binary foreground / background segmentation. Different systems are therefore easily interchangeable. As will be explained in the next chapter, we do not have any special requirements on background subtraction algorithms, but instead expect rather poor performance from them, and make our system as robust as possible to noisy and incomplete foreground masks.

2.6 Evaluation

The evaluation of a detection or tracking system is typically done by comparing the results it yields on a test sequence to the manual annotation produced by a human on the same sequence. Those results can be evaluated in terms of true and false positive rates, precision and other measures. In this work, we rely on the metrics defined by the CLEAR [115] project. We made this choice because they are widely accepted metrics for evaluating detection and tracking results. They are, among others, used by the PETS evaluation[1]. We give more details on how these metrics are computed below.

2.6.1 Ground Truth

Annotating multi-view video sequences is a time consuming process, but nevertheless an unavoidable step in any evaluation. For this work, we created two types of ground truth. First, to quantize the precision of our algorithms, we picked 100 frames at random among a complete sequence from the *laboratory* data set and marked by hand a reference point located on the belly of every person present in every camera view. Using the camera calibration, we then projected those points on the ground plane. Since the 100 frames were taken from a sequence with four individuals entering the room successively, we obtained in total 354 locations. This type of ground truth can also be used to estimate the number of detection true and false positives. However, it is not dense enough to correctly evaluate tracking algorithms, for which trajectory consistency is important.

For this purpose we created a second type of ground truth labelling that records the people position on the ground as well as their bounding boxes in camera views and their identity at a regular frame interval. The ground localization of this type

---

[1]IEEE International Workshop on Performance Evaluation of Tracking and Surveillance

of ground truth is not as precise as the previous one, but it is much faster to generate, thanks to a helper program that we specifically implemented for this purpose. Overall, we labelled the following sequences:

- a *laboratory* sequence of 3,000 frames, labeled once every 25 frames;

- a *terrace* sequence of 5,000 frames, labeled once every 25 frames;

- 4 video sequences from the *passageway* data set, measuring respectively 2,500, 800, 900 and 800 frames. These sequences were labeled once every 25 frames;

- the 800-frame long PETS 2009 sequence S2/L1, labeled once every 5 frames;

- the 11,000-frame long *behavior* test sequence, labelled once every 10 frames;

- 2 *ball* sequences, a 1,000-frame and a 1,200-frame, labelled once every 3 frames.

Note that the video data sets referred above are described in §2.7.

2.6.2   CLEAR Metrics

We give here a short overview of the CLEAR metrics used for detection and tracking evaluation. We refer the interested reader to [115, 13, 63] for a detailed description and motivations of the metrics.

2.6.2.1   Multiple Object Detection Accuracy (MODA)

MODA is a metric whose goal is to assess the accuracy of a detection system. It is a function of the missed detection (m_t) and false positive (fp_t) counts. Let $N_G^{(t)}$ denote the number of ground truth objects for a frame t. For an entire sequence, the MODA score is computed as follows:

$$\text{MODA} = 1 - \frac{\sum_{t=1}^{N_{frames}} \left(c_m(m_t) + c_f(fp_t) \right)}{\sum_{t=1}^{N_{frames}} N_G^{(t)}} \quad , \tag{2.1}$$

where c_m and c_f are two constant factors for weighting the importance of the missed detections and false positives, depending on the focus of the application. In our case, both were set to 1. N_{frames} is the total number of frames in the sequence.

2.6.2.2 Multiple Object Detection Precision (MODP)

The detection precision is evaluated using the spatial overlap between a detection and its corresponding ground truth. For this purpose, the Mapped Overlap Ratio is defined as follows:

$$\text{Mapped Overlap Ratio} = \sum_{i=1}^{N_{mapped}^{(t)}} \frac{\left|G_i^{(t)} \cap D_i^{(t)}\right|}{\left|G_i^{(t)} \cup D_i^{(t)}\right|} \quad , \tag{2.2}$$

where $G_i^{(t)}$ denotes the ith ground-truth object in the tth frame, $D_i^{(t)}$ denotes the corresponding detected object for $G_i^{(t)}$, and $N_{mapped}^{(t)}$ is the number of mapped object pairs in frame t. Note that in our multi-view case, the Mapped Overlap Ratio is also summed over all visible camera views and normalized.

The final MODP score for an entire sequence is given by the following formula:

$$\text{MODP} = \frac{\sum_{t=1}^{N_{frames}} \frac{(\text{Mapped Overlap Ratio})}{N_{mapped}^{(t)}}}{N_{frames}} \quad . \tag{2.3}$$

2.6.2.3 Multiple Object Tracking Accuracy (MOTA)

The MOTA metric is almost similar to its detection counterpart MODA. The only difference is the identity switch count per frame (isw_t) that did not exist in MODA, because it is meaningless when gauging detections. The exact formula is

$$\text{MOTA} = 1 - \frac{\sum_{t=1}^{N_{frames}} \left(c_m(m_t) + c_f(fp_t) + c_s(isw_t) \right)}{\sum_{t=1}^{N_{frames}} N_G^{(t)}} \quad , \tag{2.4}$$

where c_s is a weight function for the identity switch count. The values used for the weights in our evaluations are $c_m = c_f = 1$ and $c_s = \log_{10}$.

2.6.2.4 Multiple Object Tracking Precision (MOTP)

Finally, the MOTP metric gauges tracking precision. Here we chose the version proposed in [13], which is defined by:

$$\text{MOTP} = \frac{\sum_{t=1}^{N_{frames}} \sum_{i=1}^{N_{mapped}^{(t)}} \left[\frac{\left|G_i^{(t)} \cap D_i^{(t)}\right|}{\left|G_i^{(t)} \cup D_i^{(t)}\right|} \right]}{\sum_{t=1}^{N_{frames}} N_{mapped}^{(t)}} \quad , \tag{2.5}$$

where $N_{mapped}^{(t)}$ refers to the number of mapped object pairs in the tth frame.

2.6.2.5   True and False Positive Rates

In some of our evaluations, we also use the classical true and false positive rates. Their definition is given here for reference. Let us denote by TP, TN, FP and FN the total count of true positives, true negatives, false positives and false negatives respectively. The true positive rate is then defined as

$$TPR = \frac{TP}{TP + FN} \quad , \tag{2.6}$$

and the false positive rate as

$$FPR = \frac{FP}{FP + TN} \quad . \tag{2.7}$$

2.7   Test Data

Multi-view data sets are intrinsically difficult to acquire with temporary setups, mainly due to the amount of necessary material and the problems inherent to the simultaneous manipulation of several recording devices. Besides, in most countries, filming people in public places is subject to very strict privacy protection laws. As a result, very few multi-view pedestrian data sets are currently publicly available. A notable exception is the recent PETS 2009[2] data set, which is made of pedestrian sequences filmed from 7 different angles.

The lack of standard evaluation data motivated us to acquire our own. During the time frame of this thesis, we captured and collected multiple data sets, representing various environments in which people detection and tracking is likely to be applied. Every test environment was chosen with regard to constraints and requirements that were slightly different, such as illumination, space, etc. We have made some of our data sets publicly available online[3] in the hope that they might be useful to other researchers, and will add more in the near future.

Each set of videos, with its corresponding attributes and challenges, is briefly described below and depicted by Figs. 2.9 and 2.10. The environments' dimensions are summarized in Table 2.1.

Laboratory sequences   Those two sequences of about 2 minutes each were shot in a room of our laboratory, measuring about 7×7 m. All 4 cameras were placed in a corner of the room, at about 2 m above the ground. Four, respectively six, people enter one by one and walk continuously around the room during approximately 2

---

[2]Eleventh IEEE International Workshop on Performance Evaluation of Tracking and Surveillance, Miami, June 2009, http://pets2009.net

[3]Public multi-view pedestrian data set: http://cvlab.epfl.ch/data/pom

Environment	width	height	grid width	grid height	locations	# cam.	frame rate	image size
Laboratory	7m	7m	28	28	784	4	25	360 × 288
Laboratory w/ kids	7m	6m	30	25	750	4	25	360 × 288
Campus	12m	12m	48	48	2,304	3	25	360 × 288
Terrace	7m	10m	30	45	1,350	4	25	360 × 288
Basketball	17m	17m	64	64	4,096	5	25	720 × 576
Passageway	12m	30m	40	100	4,000	4	25	360 × 288
Behavior	10m	15m	30	44	1,320	3	25	360 × 288
PETS 09	18.5m	20m	56	61	3,416	7	7	720 × 576
Balls	80cm	52cm	60	40	2,400	1	25	600 × 400

Table 2.1: Dimensions of the areas used for pedestrian detection.

minutes. Given the relatively small size of the room, the scene appears crowded when filled with six people.

Another sequence was filmed in the same room, with a slightly different setup. This video features two adults, a 4-year-old boy and a toddler walking around in the room. This sequence was specifically acquired to show the ability of our simple pedestrian model to handle people of very different size.

Campus sequences   This set of video sequences was acquired in front of the entrance of a building on our campus. Only three cameras placed at 2 m high were used during this capture. The sequences are rather sparse, but contain some of the challenges commonly associated with outdoor environments, such as shadows, reflections and moving objects in the background.

Cafeteria terrace sequences   Several sequences of more than 3 minutes were filmed on an outdoor cafeteria terrace in our campus. Four cameras were placed at the usual 2 m high, at every corner of the area. In some of the sequences, up to 9 people appear simultaneously in front of the cameras. On other sequences, tables and chairs have been placed in the center to simulate static obstacles. The session was shot early in the morning and the sun, low on the horizon, produces very long and sharp shadows on some videos.

Passageway sequences   These sequences involve several people passing through a public underground passageway. It was captured by 4 cameras placed at every corner of the area, at 2 m above the ground. As illustrated on the first row in Fig. 2.10, this data set is very challenging for several reasons. First, lighting conditions are very poor, representative of what can be expected in a real-world surveillance situation. Most images are under-exposed, except near the exits where they often are saturated. Second, the area covered by the system is large, which means that people can get very

(a) laboratory

(b) laboratory with kids

(c) campus

(d) terrace

(e) basketball

Figure 2.9: Illustrated here are the various environments used for test purposes: (a) laboratory environment, (b) the second laboratory setup for the sequence with kids, (c) the entrance of a building on our campus, (d) a cafeteria terrace on our campus and (e) a basketball training match on half a court. The other environments are shown on Fig. 2.10.

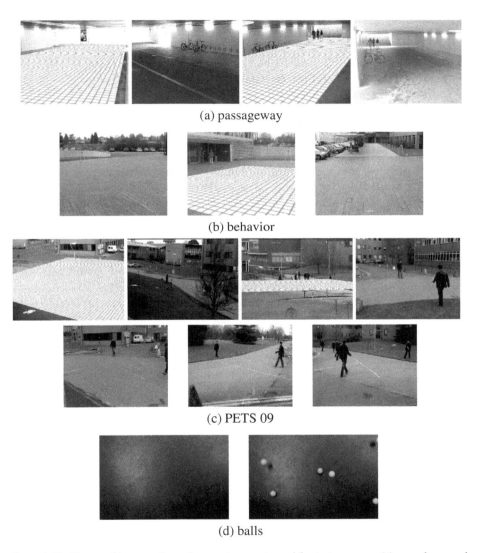

(a) passageway

(b) behavior

(c) PETS 09

(d) balls

Figure 2.10: Illustrated here are the various environments used for test purposes: (a) an underground passageway on our campus, (b) an open space in front of a building, used for behavior analysis, (c) a crossroad on the University of Reading campus, part of the PETS 09 data set and (d) multiple ping-pong balls filmed by a single camera. The other environments are shown on Fig. 2.9.

small when reaching the far end, making their precise localization challenging. Then, the ground is not perfectly flat, which makes the camera calibration suboptimal. Finally, large parts of the area of interest, especially near its edges, are seen by only two or even one camera.

Behavior sequences   This data set was acquired specifically for testing the behavior analysis algorithm introduced in Chapter 5. It was captured in front of a building on our campus by three cameras placed about 2 m above the ground. The data set is made of a test sequence and a training sequence. In the test sequence, that lasts approximatively 15 minutes, 4 people were instructed to walk according to predefined paths (see Fig. 5.6, page 136). In the 8-minute long test sequence, the same 4 people follow the patterns from the training sequence for about 50 percent of the time and take random trajectories for the rest. These random movements can include standing still for a while, going in and out of the area through non standard entrance points, taking one of the predefined trajectories backwards, etc.

Ball sequences   The ball sequences is our only data set that is not about pedestrians. It was acquired to show that our trackers can be used for completely different tasks than people tracking. Also, as opposed to most pedestrian sequences, all moving objects have exactly the same aspect and shape, making appearance models inefficient. On the two videos of the data set, 24 table tennis balls were launched across the field of view, with up to 10 appearing simultaneously on the screen. Those were filmed by a single DV camera, placed facing down about 1.5 m above the ground. The original videos were cropped to a resolution of 600×400 pixels.

PETS 2009 sequence   We use the sequence S2/L1 of the PETS 2009 data set, which is focused on multi-people tracking. The video was filmed at a road corner of the University or Reading. About 10 people are passing by. Important light changes between the background model and the sequence, as well as precision issues in camera calibration make the sequence difficult. Moreover, the sequence has been acquired at a low frame rate of 7 fps, which is an additional difficulty.

2.7.1   Material

For the acquisition of most of our sequences, standard consumer-grade DV cameras were used. Those cameras can typically record videos of 720×576 pixels at 25 frames per second, during about one hour. This setup was chosen for its convenience and versatility. DV cameras are usually small and light, and can be quickly installed almost anywhere with tripods. Using independent cameras sacrifices the possibility of automatic stream synchronization. However, this was not an insolvable issue, and we were able to rather easily synchronize the streams by hand during post processing. Fortunately, we found the camera's frame rate to be very stable, even across different brands, and our sequences did not suffer from frame drift. For our applications the DV resolution was unnecessarily high, and all our sequences shot with DV cameras were downsampled by a factor of 2, to a resolution of 360×288. This also got rid of annoying interlacing effects. Among our data sets, the following were filmed with DV: *laboratory with kids, campus, terrace, passageway, behavior* and *balls*.

The *basketball* data set was filmed with semi-professional HDV cameras, with a native resolution of $1,440 \times 1,080$ pixels and an aspect ratio of 16:9. It was later downsampled to DV resolution of 720×576, which gives it its stretched aspect ratio. The stream's frame rate is 25 fps, and synchronization was also realized manually.

The *laboratory* data set was filmed with a dedicated video surveillance setup, which includes 4 analog CCTV cameras connected to a PC via a video acquisition board. The cameras deliver a resolution of 360×288 pixels at 25 frames per second. This setup is convenient because all streams are acquired synchronously and directly stored on a hard-drive. Furthermore, it can be used for real time processing. Despite its obvious advantages, this setup was only used for filming the indoor *laboratory* scene, because it is too cumbersome to be installed anywhere else.

Finally, the PETS 2009 data set was acquired by a mixed network of cameras comprising 4 standard DV cameras and 3 Axis network cameras with a resolution of 768×576 pixels. While the DV frame rate is 25 fps, the network cameras had a lower one of about 7 fps. The publicly available videos have all been downsampled to a common 7 fps frame rate.

Chapter 3

People Detection and Localization

In this chapter, we present two complementary approaches to tackle the multi-person detection problem. The first one, dubbed POM for *Probabilistic Occupancy Map*, operates on background subtraction images, and uses a generative model to recursively estimate the probabilities of a discrete occupancy grid. The second approach replaces the background subtraction by an image-based pedestrian detector, in an attempt to bypass limitations of the first method.

3.1 State-of-the-Art

State-of-the-art approaches to people detection can be roughly divided into monocular and multi-view categories.

3.1.1 Monocular Approaches

Monocular approaches rely on the input of a single camera to perform detection. These methods provide a simple and easy-to-deploy setup, but must compensate for the lack of 3-D information of a single camera view. In general, monocular people detection methods look at various locations of the input image and try to determine whether the sub-window shall be assigned to the pedestrian or non-pedestrian class, depending on the corresponding class posterior probability. They can be categorized into *generative* or *discriminative* approaches, from the way the posterior probabilities are estimated for each class.

31

3.1.1.1   Generative Models

Generative approaches to pedestrian classification model the appearance of the pedestrian class in terms of its class-conditional density function. In combination with the class priors, the posterior probability for the pedestrian class can be inferred using a Bayesian approach [35].

Several approaches rely on background subtraction to obtain an initial guess about the potential location of people and then use shape analysis to validate the correct hypotheses. Methods are diverse and include vertical and horizontal histogram projection of silhouettes [48], mean-shift algorithm for correct blob size selection [22], ellipse fitting of background subtraction blobs [143], template matching based on the Chamfer distance transform [41] or Marked Point Process to explain background blobs with a set of previously learned silhouettes [43].

Other approaches combine shape and texture models, in order to obtain a richer representation. Examples are [57], which uses the CONDENSATION [56] algorithm with human shape model and the constraints given by camera calibration to track multiple people. [37] learns a statistical pedestrian image model from examples, using PCA. A model image can then be reconstructed as a linear combination of the eigenvectors extracted from the training images. In [44], multi-cue 3-D object tracking is addressed by combining particle-filter based Bayesian tracking and detection using learnt spatio-temporal shapes. [46] merges cues from the original image, foreground masks and a neural-network based pedestrian detector.

Some work that track in a single view prior to computing correspondences across views extend this approach to multi camera setups. However, we view them as falling into the same category because they do not simultaneously exploit the information from multiple views. In [20], a background/foreground segmentation is performed on calibrated images, followed by human shape distinction from segmented foreground objects and feature point extraction from the selected blobs. Feature points are tracked in a single view and the system switches to another view when the current camera no longer has a good view of the person. In [66], the limits of the field of view of each camera are computed in every other camera from motion information. When a person becomes visible in one camera, the system automatically searches for him in other views where he should be visible.

3.1.1.2   Discriminative Models

In contrast to the generative models, discriminative models approximate the Bayesian maximum-a-posteriori decision by learning the parameters of a discriminant function between the pedestrian and non-pedestrian classes from training examples [35].

Approaches mainly differ by the image features they are using for classification. Typical examples are non-adaptive Haar wavelet features [127], code-book feature patches [75], edgelet features [132] or histogram of gradients [26, 145].

Various classifier architectures have also been tried, such as convolutional neural network [118], Support Vector Machines [26] and AdaBoost using boosted detector cascades [127, 132, 145].

Yet another class of monocular pedestrian detectors have tried to break down the complex appearance of a human into easier smaller parts. Those approaches usually rely on a mixture of experts and train specialized experts for each sub-part [91, 110, 141].

3.1.2 Multi-View Approaches

Despite the effectiveness of monocular methods, the use of multiple cameras soon becomes necessary when one wishes to accurately detect and track multiple people and compute their precise 3-D locations in a complex environment. Occlusion handling is facilitated by using two sets of stereo color cameras [71]. However, in most approaches that only take a set of 2-D views as input, occlusion is mainly handled by imposing temporal consistency on the detections, in terms of a motion model, be it Kalman filtering or more general Markov models. As a result, these approaches may not always be able to recover if the process starts diverging.

Compared to monocular approaches, multi-view ones have to deal with the additional challenge of registering the different camera views. In pedestrian detection and tracking, people are often assumed to walk on a flat ground plane, and it is therefore sufficient to compute homographies mapping the ground plane between different camera views [64, 68, 65, 36, 28]. More complex world model sometimes necessitates full camera calibration [86, 87, 96].

A majority of approaches start by performing background subtraction on individual camera views to locate the moving parts [136, 96, 68, 64, 39, 1]. The obtained background blobs from all cameras are then merged using various methods, often relying on 3-D cues from camera calibration.

In [136], a ground occupancy map is computed with a standard visual hull procedure from the motion segmentation images. One originality of the approach is to keep for each resulting connected component an upper and lower bound on the number of objects it can contain. Based on motion consistency, the bounds on the various components are estimated at a certain time frame based on the bounds of the components at the previous time frame that spatially intersect with it.

In [96] a recursive Bayesian estimation approach is used to deal with occlusions while tracking multiple people in multi-view. The algorithm tracks objects located in the intersections of 2-D visual angles, which are extracted from silhouettes obtained from different fixed views. When occlusion ambiguities occur, multiple occlusion hypotheses are generated given predicted object states and previous hypotheses, and tested using a branch-and-merge strategy. The proposed framework is implemented using a customized particle filter to represent the distribution of object states.

[64, 65] projects the foreground blobs onto the ground plane using homographies. The projections coming from all cameras are multiplied, which yields the position of the pedestrian's feet. [97] follows the same approach for people and vehicles detection. Foreground blobs are segmented in individual views prior to being projected and intersected in the ground plane. [36] proceeds in a relatively similar manner, but projects the silhouettes on the head plane instead, and thus retrieves people's head position. This modification can be useful in case of denser crowds. [28] extends the methods by projecting the blobs to several planes parallel to the ground at various heights, and propose a heuristic-based method to combine the multiple projections thus generated.

[52, 68] first label individual background blobs using updated color models, and, for each blob, compute its vertical axis. Axes from every view are projected on the ground and expected to intersect at a single point.

[1] uses a generative model of the background subtraction based on semi-elliptical silhouettes and searches for the ground occupancy map that maximizes the fit of the generated images with the original foreground blobs, while respecting a sparsity constraint.

Besides the various methods relying initially on background subtraction, some have chosen to work directly on image features. [87] proposes a system that segments, detects and tracks multiple people in a scene using a wide-baseline setup of up to 16 synchronized cameras. Intensity information is directly used to perform single-view pixel classification and match similarly labeled regions across views to derive 3-D people locations. Occlusion analysis is performed in two ways. First, during pixel classification, the computation of prior probabilities takes occlusion into account. Second, evidence is gathered across cameras to compute a presence likelihood map on the ground plane that accounts for the visibility of each ground plane point in each view. [89] proposes a method based on dimensionality reduction to learn a correspondence between appearance of pedestrians across several views. This approach is able to cope with severe occlusion in one view by exploiting the appearance of the same pedestrian on another view and the consistency across views.

3.2 People Detection with a Probabilistic Occupancy Map

In this section, we present a first multi-view people detection algorithm called POM[1] for *Probabilistic Occupancy Map*. It estimates the probabilities of occupancy of the ground plane given the binary images obtained from the input images via background subtraction [39]. The algorithm only takes into account images acquired at the *same*

---

[1]An open-source version of the POM people detection algorithm is available under GPL license at http://cvlab.epfl.ch/software/pom/.

Table 3.1: Notation (deterministic quantities)

$W \times H$	image resolution.
C	number of cameras.
K	number of locations in the ground discretization ($\simeq 1000$).
$I \otimes J$	intersection of images, $\forall (x,y), (I \otimes J)(x,y) = I(x,y)J(x,y)$.
$I \oplus J$	disjunction of images, $\forall (x,y), (I \oplus J)(x,y) = 1 - (1 - I(x,y))(1 - J(x,y))$.
Ψ	a pseudo-distance between images.
Q	the product law used to approximate, for a fixed t, the real posterior distribution $P(\cdot \mid \mathbf{B}_t)$.
E_Q	Expectation under $\mathbf{X} \sim Q$.
q_k	the marginal probability of Q, that is $Q(X^k = 1)$.
ε_k	the prior probability of presence at location k, $P(X^k = 1)$.
λ_k	is $\log \frac{1 - \varepsilon_k}{\varepsilon_k}$, the log-ratio of the prior probability.
$\mathscr{A}_k^c$	the image composed of 1s inside a rectangle standing for the silhouette of an individual at location k seen from camera c, and 0s elsewhere.

time by the multiple cameras. Its basic ingredient is a generative model, that represents humans as simple rectangles, and is used to create synthetic ideal images we would observe if people were at given locations. Under this model of the image given the true occupancy, we approximate the probabilities of occupancy at every location as the marginals of a product law minimizing the Kullback-Leibler divergence [72] from the "true" conditional posterior distribution. This allows us to evaluate the probabilities of occupancy at every location as the fixed point of a large system of equations.

This represents a departure from more classical approaches to estimating probabilities of occupancy that rely on computing a visual hull [136]. Such approaches tend to be pessimistic and do not exploit trade-offs between the presences of people at different locations. For instance, if due to noise in one camera, a person is not seen in a particular view, he would be discarded even if he were seen in all others. By contrast, in our probabilistic framework, sufficient evidence might be present to detect him. Similarly, the presence of someone at a specific location creates an occlusion that hides the presence behind, which is not accounted for by the hull techniques but is by our approach.

Recall that we partition the visible area of the ground plane into a regular grid of K locations as shown in Figures 3.1(c) and 3.2. Let X_t^k be a Boolean random variable standing for the presence of an individual at location k of the grid at time t, and $\mathbf{X}_t$ the random vector $(X_t^1, \ldots, X_t^K)$ standing for the occupancy of the whole grid at time

Table 3.2: Notation (random quantities)

$\mathbf{I}_t$	images from all the cameras $\mathbf{I}_t = (I_t^1, \ldots, I_t^C)$.
$\mathbf{B}_t$	binary images generated by the background subtraction $\mathbf{B}_t = (B_t^1, \ldots, B_t^C)$.
A_t^c	ideal random image generated by putting rectangles $\mathscr{A}_k^c$ where $X_t^k = 1$, thus a function of $\mathbf{X}_t$.
$\overline{A}_{k,\xi}^c$	compact notation for the average synthetic image $E_Q(A^c \mid X^k = \xi)$, see Figure 3.2.
$\mathbf{X}_t$	vectors of boolean random variable $(X_t^1, \ldots, X_t^K)$ standing for the occupancy of location k on the ground plane.

t. From the input images $\mathbf{I}_t$, we use background subtraction to produce binary masks $\mathbf{B}_t$, such as those of Fig. 3.1(b). Tables 3.1 and 3.2 summarize the notation used throughout this section.

To estimate accurately the probabilities of presence at every location, we need to take into account both the information provided in each separate view and the couplings between views produced by occlusions. Instead of combining heuristics related to geometrical consistency or sensor noise, we encompass all the available prior information we have about the task in a generative model of the result of the background subtraction, given the true state of occupancy $(X_t^1, \ldots, X_t^K)$ we are trying to estimate.

Ideally, provided with such a model of $P(\mathbf{B}_t \mid \mathbf{X}_t)$, that is of the result of the background subtraction given the true state of occupancy of the scene, estimating $P(\mathbf{X}_t \mid \mathbf{B}_t)$ becomes a Bayesian computation. However, due to the complexity of any non-trivial model of $P(\mathbf{B}_t \mid \mathbf{X}_t)$ and to the dimensionality of both $\mathbf{B}_t$ and $\mathbf{X}_t$, this cannot be done with a generic method.

To address this problem, we represent humans as simple rectangles and use them to create synthetic ideal images we would observe if people were at given locations. Under this model of the image given the true state, we approximate the occupancy probabilities $P(X_t^k = 1 \mid \mathbf{B}_t)$ as the marginals $q_k = Q(X_k^t = 1)$ of a product law Q minimizing the Kullback-Leibler divergence from the "true" conditional posterior distribution. This allows us to compute these probabilities as the fixed point of a large system of equations.

More specifically, in Section §3.2.1 we introduce two independence assumptions, under which we derive the analytical results of the other sections, and argue that they are legitimate. In Section §3.2.2 we propose our generative model of $P(\mathbf{B} \mid \mathbf{X})$, which involves measuring the distance between the actual images $\mathbf{B}$ and a crude synthetic image that is a function of the $\mathbf{X}$. From these assumptions and model, we derive in Section §3.2.3 an analytical relation between estimates $q_1, \ldots, q_K$ of the marginal probabilities of occupancy $P(X_t^1 = 1 \mid \mathbf{B}_t), \dots, P(X_t^K = 1 \mid \mathbf{B}_t)$ by minimizing the Kullback-Leibler divergence between the corresponding product law and the true posterior. This leads to a fast iterative algorithm that estimates them as the solution of a fixed point problem, as shown in Section §3.2.4.

Since we perform these steps at each time frame separately, we drop t from all notations in the remainder of this section for clarity.

3.2.1 Independence Assumptions

We introduce here two assumptions of independence that will allow us to derive analytically the relation between the optimal q_ks.

Our first assumption is that individuals in the room do not take into account the presence of other individuals in their vicinity when moving around, which is true as long as avoidance strategies and other social norms are ignored. This can be formalized as

$$P(X^1, \dots, X^K) = \prod_k P(X^k). \tag{3.1}$$

Our second assumption involves considering that all statistical dependencies between views are due to the presence of individuals in the room. This is equivalent to treating the views as functions of the vector $\mathbf{X} = (X^1, \dots, X^K)$ plus some independent noise. This implies that, as soon as the presence of all individuals is known, the views become independent. This is true as long as we ignore other hidden variables such as morphology or garments, that may simultaneously influence several views. This assumption can be written down as

$$P(B^1, \dots, B^C \mid \mathbf{X}) = \prod_c P(B^c \mid \mathbf{X}). \tag{3.2}$$

3.2.2 Generative Image Model

To relate the values of the X^ks to the images produced by background subtraction $B^1, \dots, B^C$, we propose here a model of the latter given the former.

Following the silhouette model introduced in Chapter 2.3, human blobs are approximated by rectangles of ratio 2:7, and we denote by $\mathscr{A}_k^c$ the image composed of 1s inside a rectangle standing for the silhouette of an individual at location k seen from camera c, and 0s elsewhere. Let A^c be the synthetic image obtained by putting rectangles at locations where $X^k = 1$, thus $A^c = \oplus_k X^k \mathscr{A}_k^c$, where $\oplus$ denotes the "union" between two images. An example of synthetic image is shown in Fig. 3.2.a. Such an image is a function of $\mathbf{X}$ and thus a random quantity. We model the image B^c produced by the background subtraction as if it was this ideal image with some random noise.

As it appears empirically that the noise increases with the area of the ideal image A^c, we introduce a normalized pseudo-distance Ψ to account for this asymmetry. For any gray-scale image $A \in [0,1]^{W \times H}$ we denote by $|A|$ the sum of its pixels, and we denote by $\otimes$ the product per-pixel of two images. We introduce Ψ defined by

$$\forall B, A \in [0,1]^{W \times H}, \quad \Psi(B,A) = \frac{1}{\sigma} \frac{|B \otimes (1-A) + (1-B) \otimes A|}{|A|}. \tag{3.3}$$

and we model the conditional distribution $P(B^c \,|\, \mathbf{X})$ of the background subtraction images given the true hidden state as a density decreasing with the pseudo-distance $\Psi(B^c, A^c)$ between the image produced by the background subtraction and an image A^c obtained by putting rectangular shapes where people are present according to $\mathbf{X}$. We end up with the following model

$$P(\mathbf{B} \,|\, \mathbf{X}) \;=\; \prod_c P(B^c \,|\, \mathbf{X}) \tag{3.4}$$

$$=\; \prod_c P(B^c \,|\, A^c) \tag{3.5}$$

$$=\; \frac{1}{Z} \prod_c e^{-\Psi(B^c, A^c)}. \tag{3.6}$$

The parameter σ accounts for the quality of the background subtraction. The smaller σ the more B^c is picked around its ideal value A^c. The value of σ was fixed arbitrarily to 0.01, but experiments demonstrated that the algorithm is not very sensitive to that value.

3.2.3 Relation between the q_ks

Having introduced a generative model of $P(\mathbf{B} \,|\, \mathbf{X})$, we now look for an approximation of $P(X^k = 1 \,|\, \mathbf{B})$. Our strategy is to estimate it with a product law $Q(\mathbf{X}) = \prod_k Q(X^k)$, by minimizing the Kullback-Leibler divergence [72] between the two probability distributions.

Recall that the Kullback-Leibler divergence between two distributions R and S is defined as

$$KL(R, S) = \sum_y R(y) \log \frac{R(y)}{S(y)} = E_R \left(\log \frac{R(Y)}{S(Y)} \right), \tag{3.7}$$

where E_R represents the expectation under $\mathbf{Y} \sim R$. To minimize the Kullback-Leibler divergence between the product law Q and the true conditional law on $\mathbf{X}$ given $\mathbf{B}$, we derive it with respect to the unknown q_k

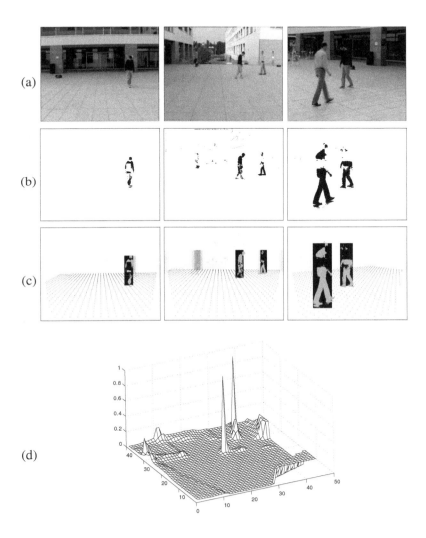

Figure 3.1: Original images from three cameras (a), binary blobs produced by background subtraction (b) and synthetic average images computed from them by the estimation of the probabilistic occupancy map (POM) algorithm (c). The graph (d) represents the corresponding occupancy probabilities q_k on the grid.

$$\frac{\partial}{\partial q_k} KL(Q, P(\,\cdot\,|\mathbf{B}))$$

$$= \frac{\partial}{\partial q_k} E_Q\left(\log\frac{Q(\mathbf{X})}{P(\mathbf{X}|\mathbf{B})}\right) \tag{3.8}$$

$$= \frac{\partial}{\partial q_k} E_Q\left(\log\frac{Q(\mathbf{X})\,P(\mathbf{B})}{P(\mathbf{X})P(\mathbf{B}|\mathbf{X})}\right) \tag{3.9}$$

$$= \frac{\partial}{\partial q_k} E_Q\left(\sum_l \log\frac{Q(X^l)}{P(X^l)} + \log P(\mathbf{B}) - \log P(\mathbf{B}|\mathbf{X})\right) \tag{3.10}$$

$$= \frac{\partial}{\partial q_k} E_Q\left(\log\frac{Q(X^k)}{P(X^k)} - \log P(\mathbf{B}|\mathbf{X})\right) \tag{3.11}$$

$$= \frac{\partial}{\partial q_k} q_k\left(\log\frac{q_k}{\varepsilon_k} - E_Q\left(\log P(\mathbf{B}|\mathbf{X})\,|\,X^k = 1\right)\right)$$
$$\quad + \frac{\partial}{\partial q_k} (1-q_k)\left(\log\frac{1-q_k}{1-\varepsilon_k} - E_Q\left(\log P(\mathbf{B}|\mathbf{X})\,|\,X^k = 0\right)\right) \tag{3.12}$$

$$= \log\frac{q_k}{\varepsilon_k} + 1 - E_Q\left(\log P(\mathbf{B}|\mathbf{X})\,|\,X^k = 1\right)$$
$$\quad - \log\frac{1-q_k}{1-\varepsilon_k} - 1 + E_Q\left(\log P(\mathbf{B}|\mathbf{X})\,|\,X^k = 0\right) \tag{3.13}$$

$$= \log\frac{q_K\,(1-\varepsilon_k)}{(1-q_k)\,\varepsilon_k} - E_Q\left(\log P(\mathbf{B}|\mathbf{X})\,|\,X^k = 1\right)$$
$$\quad + E_Q\left(\log P(\mathbf{B}|\mathbf{X})\,|\,X^k = 0\right)$$

$$= \log\frac{q_K\,(1-\varepsilon_k)}{(1-q_k)\,\varepsilon_k} - E_Q\left(-\sum_c \Psi(B^c, A^c)\,\middle|\,X^k = 1\right)$$
$$\quad + E_Q\left(-\sum_c \Psi(B^c, A^c)\,\middle|\,X^k = 0\right) \tag{3.14}$$

Equality (3.8) is the definition of the Kullback-Leibler divergence, (3.9) is obtained by applying Bayes's rule to $P(\mathbf{X}|\mathbf{B})$. Equality (3.10) is true under our assumption of independence of the X^ks and (3.11) by removing terms which are constant with respect to q_k. We develop the expectation by conditioning on X^k to get (3.12), do formal differentiation to obtain (3.13), and finally introduce our model of $P(\mathbf{B}|\mathbf{X})$ and assumption of conditional independence of the B^c given $\mathbf{X}$ to get (3.14).

Hence, if we solve

$$\frac{\partial}{\partial q_k} KL(Q, P(\,\cdot\,|\mathbf{B})) = 0 \tag{3.15}$$

we obtain

$$q_k = \frac{1}{1 + \exp\left(\lambda_k + \sum_c E_Q(\Psi(B^c, A^c) \mid X^k = 1) - E_Q(\Psi(B^c, A^c) \mid \mathbf{X}) \mid X^k = 0)\right)}, \quad (3.16)$$

with $\lambda_k = \log \frac{1 - \varepsilon_k}{\varepsilon_k}$.

Unfortunately, the computation of $E_Q(\Psi(B^c, A^c) \mid X^k = \xi)$ is untractable. However, since under $\mathbf{X} \sim Q$ the image A^c is concentrated around B^c, we approximate, $\forall \xi \in \{0, 1\}$

$$E_Q(\Psi(B^c, A^c) \mid X^k = \xi) \simeq \Psi(B^c, E_Q(A^c \mid X^k = \xi)) \quad (3.17)$$

leading to our main result

$$q_k = \frac{1}{1 + \exp\left(\lambda_k + \sum_c \Psi(B^c, E_Q(A^c \mid X^k = 1)) - \Psi(B^c, E_Q(A^c \mid X^k = 0))\right)}. \quad (3.18)$$

Note that the conditional synthetic images $E_Q(A^c \mid X^k = 0)$ and $E_Q(A^c \mid X^k = 1)$ are equal to $E_Q(A^c)$ with q_k forced to 0 or 1 respectively, as shown on Fig. 3.2. Since Q is a product law, we have for any pixel (x, y)

$$E_Q(A^c(x, y)) = Q(A^c(x, y) = 1) \quad (3.19)$$
$$= 1 - Q(\forall k, \mathscr{A}_k^c(x, y) X^k = 0) \quad (3.20)$$
$$= 1 - \prod_{k: \mathscr{A}_k^c(x,y)=1} (1 - q_k). \quad (3.21)$$

Finally, $E_Q(A^c \mid X^k = \xi)$ are functions of the $(q_l)_{l \neq k}$ and Equation (3.18) can be seen as one equation of a large system whose unknowns are the q_ks. Fig. 3.5 shows the evolution of both the marginals q_k and the average images $E_Q(A^c)$ during the iterative estimation of the solution.

Intuitively, if putting the rectangular shape for position k in the image improves the fit with the actual images, the score $\Psi(B^c, E_Q(A^c \mid X^k = 1))$ decreases, while $\Psi(B^c, E_Q(A^c \mid X^k = 0))$ increases, and the sum in the exponential in (3.18) becomes negative, leading to a larger q_k. A concrete example is shown in Fig. 3.3: For simplicity, only one camera view is considered. Images (b) and (c) represent two conditional synthetic images used for the estimation of the occupancy probability q_k of location k. Obviously, $\overline{A}_{k,1}^c$ is closer to the foreground image than $\overline{A}_{k,0}^c$, and thus the distance $\Psi(B^c, \overline{A}_{k,1}^c)$ is smaller than $\Psi(B^c, \overline{A}_{k,0}^c)$. This in turn implies that the exponential part in Equation (3.18) is negative, leading to a value of q_k close to 1.

Note that occlusion is taken into account naturally: If a rectangular shape at position k is occluded by another one whose presence is very likely, the value of q_k does not influence the average image and all terms vanish but λ_k in the exponential.

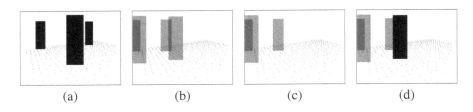

(a)   (b)   (c)   (d)

Figure 3.2: Picture (a) shows a synthetic picture A^c with three X^ks equal to 1. Picture (b) shows the average image $E_Q(A^c)$ where all q_k are null but four of them equal to 0.2. Pictures (c) and (d) show $\overline{A}^c_{k,0} = E_Q(A^c \mid X^k = 0)$ and $\overline{A}^c_{k,1} = E_Q(A^c \mid X^k = 1)$ respectively, where k is the location corresponding to the black rectangle in (d).

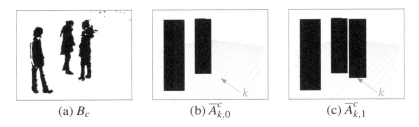

(a) B_c (b) $\overline{A}^c_{k,0}$ (c) $\overline{A}^c_{k,1}$

Figure 3.3: Illustration of POM's generative model. For a given foreground image (a), images (b) and (c) represent two possible average synthetic images in which the occupancy probability of location k is respectively forced to 0 and 1. In this particular case, (c) is obviously closer to the foreground image than (b) and thus $\Psi(B^c, \overline{A}^c_{k,0}) > \Psi(B^c, \overline{A}^c_{k,1})$. According to Equation (3.18), q_k will thus be estimated to a value close to 1.

Thus the resulting q_k remains equal to the prior. This fact is illustrated in Fig. 3.4: since location l is almost completely occluded, the two conditional synthetic images $\overline{A}^c_{l,0}$ and $\overline{A}^c_{l,1}$ are very similar. Logically, their respective distances to the foreground image $\Psi(B^c, \overline{A}^c_{l,0})$ and $\Psi(B^c, \overline{A}^c_{l,1})$ are almost equal and cancel out in the exponential part of Equation (3.18). Thus, the value q_l becomes

$$q_l \simeq \frac{1}{1 + \exp \lambda_l} = \varepsilon_l \,, \tag{3.22}$$

which corresponds to the prior probability of occupancy. This result makes sense: When a location is occluded on a camera view, the corresponding foreground image provides no information about its occupancy. Therefore, the q_l should be set to the prior probability.

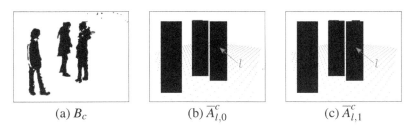

(a) B_c (b) $\overline{A}_{l,0}^c$ (c) $\overline{A}_{l,1}^c$

Figure 3.4: Illustration of POM's handling of occlusions. Images (b) and (c) represent two possible average synthetic images corresponding to the foreground image (a), where location l is almost completely occluded. Since images (b) and (c) are very similar, $\Psi(B^c, \overline{A}_{l,0}^c) \simeq \Psi(B^c, \overline{A}_{l,1}^c)$. As a result, the estimate of q_l from Equation (3.18) is close to the prior probability ε_l. This result makes sense: When provided with no information about a location's occupancy, it is estimated to the occupancy prior.

3.2.4 Fast Estimation of the q_ks

We estimate the q_k as follows: We first give them a uniform value and use them to compute the average synthetic images $\overline{A}_{k,\xi}^c = E_Q(A^c | X^k = \xi)$. We then re-estimate every q_k with Equation (3.18) and iterate the process until a stable solution is reached.

The main remaining issue is the computation of $\Psi(B^c, \overline{A}_{k,\xi}^c)$ which has to be done K times per iteration for as many iterations as required to converge, which is usually of the order of 100.

Fortunately, the images $E_Q(A^c)$ and $\overline{A}_{k,\xi}^c$ differ only in the rectangle $\mathscr{A}_k$, where the latter is multiplied by a constant factor. Hence, we can show that by using integral images [126] we can compute the distance from the true image produced by the background subtraction to the average image obtained with one of the q_k modified at constant time and very rapidly.

We organize the computation to take advantage of that trick, and finally perform the following steps at each iteration of our algorithm.

Let $\oplus$ denote the pixel-wise disjunction operator between binary images (the "union" image), $\otimes$ the pixel-wise product (the "intersection" image), $|I|$ the sum of the pixels of an image I and let 1 be the constant image whose pixels are all equal to 1.

$$\overline{A}^c = 1 - \otimes_k \left(1 - q_k \mathscr{A}_k^c\right) \tag{3.23}$$

$$|\overline{A}_{k,\xi}^c| = |\overline{A}^c| + \frac{\xi - q_k}{1 - q_k} |(1 - \overline{A}^c) \otimes \mathscr{A}_k^c| \tag{3.24}$$

$$|B_c \otimes \overline{A}_{k,\xi}^c| = |B_c \otimes \overline{A}^c| + \frac{\xi - q_k}{1 - q_k} |B_c \otimes \left(1 - \overline{A}^c\right) \otimes \mathscr{A}_k^c| \tag{3.25}$$

$$\Psi(B_c, \overline{A}_{k,\xi}^c) = \frac{1}{\sigma} \frac{|B_c| - 2 |B_c \otimes \overline{A}_{k,\xi}^c| + |\overline{A}_{k,\xi}^c|}{|\overline{A}_{k,\xi}^c|} \tag{3.26}$$

$$q_k \leftarrow \frac{1}{1 + \exp\left(\lambda_k + \sum_c \Psi(B_c, \overline{A}_{k,1}^c) - \Psi(B_c, \overline{A}_{k,0}^c)\right)} \tag{3.27}$$

At each iteration and for every c, step (3.23) involves computing the average of the synthetic image under Q with the current estimates of q_ks. Steps (3.24) and (3.25) respectively sum the pixels of the conditional average images, given X^k, and of the same image multiplied pixel-wise by the output of the background subtraction. This is done at the same time for every k and uses pre-computed integral images of $1 - \overline{A}^c$ and $B_c \otimes \left(1 - \overline{A}^c\right)$) respectively. Finally, steps (3.26) and (3.27) return the distance between the result of the background subtraction and the conditional average synthetic image under Q, and the corresponding updated marginal probability. Except for the exponential in the last step, which has to be repeated at every location, the computation only involves sums and products and is therefore fast.

3.2.5 Alternate Generative Model

As mentioned in Chapter 2.3, our silhouette model is specifically tailored for modelling pedestrian silhouettes viewed from an angle that matches our camera setup. However, the POM detector is a very generic algorithm and can be easily adapted to completely different applications. We show here how we adapted the silhouette model to the monocular detection of multiple table tennis balls.

As opposed to people, balls project a simple and constant circular shape in images. The balls from our sequences are bouncing on the ground and their size slightly changes as they move closer to the camera. This effect is minimal though, and we can reasonably approximate their size as fixed. A disc would therefore be an obvious model. However, we instead approximate the balls' shape with squares, to be able to use integral images in our computations. This simple silhouette model is illustrated in Fig. 3.6. Because the camera is perpendicular to the ground plane, it is in fact filming a top view, so no camera calibration is needed to relate the occupancy map to the ground plane.

The adaptation of the silhouette model is the only required change to use POM on the balls sequence. Going from multi-view to monocular is completely natural:

Figure 3.5: Convergence process for the estimation of the probabilistic occupancy map. Camera views show both background subtraction blobs (in green) and the synthetic average image corresponding to different iterations. On the right most column are the top view probabilistic occupancy maps, with the camera fields of view.

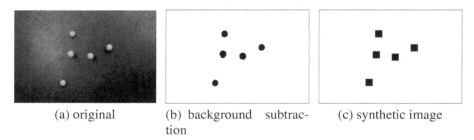

(a) original   (b) background subtrac-   (c) synthetic image
                        tion

Figure 3.6: The silhouettes model adapted to the monocular table tennis balls environment. The rectangular human silhouettes whose size was determined by camera calibration are simply replaced by squares of fixed size.

the number of cameras C is variable and can take any values, including 1. Thus, the sum over the cameras in Equation (3.18) disappears and the marginal probabilities of presence q_k are simply updated as follows:

$$q_k = \frac{1}{1 + \exp\left(\lambda_k + \Psi(B, E_Q(A \mid X^k = 1)) - \Psi(B, E_Q(A \mid X^k = 0)))\right)}. \tag{3.28}$$

The same procedure applies when treating monocular pedestrian sequences.

3.2.6 Results

In this section, we showcase the POM detector on various different environments. Its performance is evaluated with standard metrics for object detection on our multi-view pedestrian data set described in Chapter 2.7. We also study the influence of several parameters on the detector's accuracy.

3.2.6.1 Evaluation

Figure 3.7 displays detection results on the labelled sequences, evaluated with the CLEAR [115] metrics. POM's performance varies between sequences, as a function of the scene difficulty. Although relatively crowded, the *laboratory* and *terrace* sequences have a precise calibration and reasonably good lighting, which yields excellent detection scores. With their very poor lighting, the *passageway* sequences obtain a lower score. So does the PETS sequence, which suffers from uneven ground plane and non-optimal calibration. POM's results have been publicly evaluated on the PETS 09 data set and compared to other state-of-the-art detection algorithms in [12, 34]. In this ranking, our algorithm compares very favorably to other approaches, as illustrated by Fig. 4.19, page 117. Example detection results are depicted by Figs. 3.8 (*laboratory* sequence), 3.9 (*campus* sequence), 3.10 (*terrace* sequences), 3.11 (*PETS 2009* sequence), 3.12 (*passageway* sequences) and 3.13 (*basketball* sequence). Note that the two last rows of Fig. 3.10 demonstrate the ability of our algorithm to handle small obstacles as well as strong shadows. A careful observation of the corresponding occupancy maps reveals that they are less clean than correctly lighted environments, potentially leading to false positives.

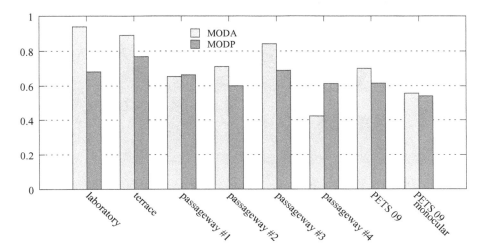

Figure 3.7: Detection results on various sequences, evaluated with the CLEAR [115] detection metrics for accuracy (MODA) and precision (MODP).

Figure 3.8: Detection results on the *laboratory* sequence. Every row shows a different time frame. The first 4 columns each displays another camera view, while the right column depicts the occupancy map.

Figure 3.9: Detection results on the *campus* sequence. Every row shows a different time frame. The first 3 columns each displays another camera view, while the right column depicts the occupancy map.

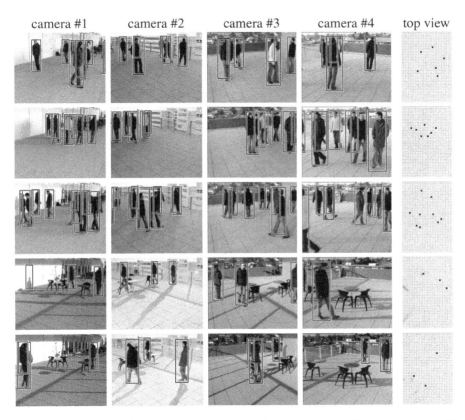

Figure 3.10: Detection results on the *terrace* sequence. Every row shows a different time frame. The first 4 columns each displays another camera view, while the right column depicts the occupancy map. Note that, despite the strong shadows, POM still correctly locates people in the two last rows. On the fourth row, a false positive is visible on camera #1, due to a shadow projected on a wall.

Figure 3.11: Detection results on the *PETS 2009* sequence. Every row shows a different time frame. The first 4 columns display 4 of the 5 camera views used for detection, while the right column depicts the occupancy map.

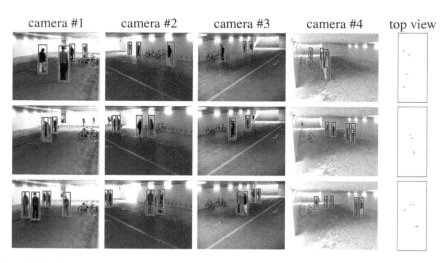

Figure 3.12: Detection results on the *passageway* sequence. Every row shows a different time frame. The first 4 columns each displays another camera view, while the right column depicts the occupancy map.

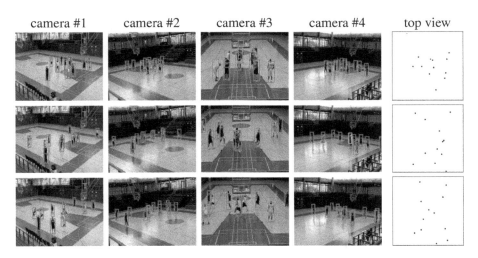

Figure 3.13: Detection results on the *basketball* sequence. Every row shows a different time frame. The first 4 columns display 4 of the 5 camera views used for detection, while the right column depicts the occupancy map. Note that the ball does not affect the detection quality. A ball is a small object compared to a human silhouette. It thus only acts as noise on background subtraction images and does not interfere with the detection algorithm.

Figure 3.14: Monocular detection results on the *PETS 2009* sequence. The first row shows camera view bounding boxes at different frames, while the second row displays the occupancy maps.

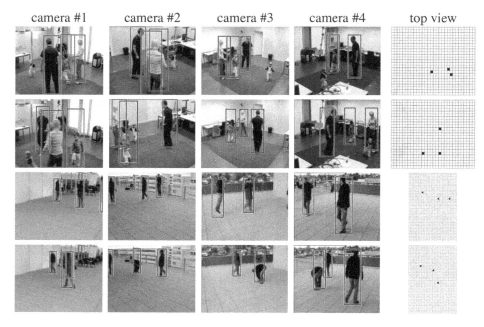

Figure 3.15: Various results from the *laboratory* and *terrace* data sets, showing that despite the fixed size and aspect ratio of the rectangle used for pedestrian approximation, our detector is not affected by people of different size, or unusual body poses (such as people jumping or bending in the last two rows of the figure).

In the rest of this section, we shed light on the influence of some parameters on the quality of detection results.

Rectangle Projection Size   In our generative model, human silhouettes are approximated by rectangles of size ratio 7:2 and height 175 cm. This number was chosen because it roughly corresponds to the average people size in current western societies.

We checked the influence of the size of the rectangular shapes we use as models: The results are almost unchanged for model sizes between 1.7 m and 2.2 m. The performance tends to decrease for sizes noticeably smaller. This can be explained easily: If the model is shorter than the person, the algorithm will be more sensitive to spurious binary blobs that it may explain by locating a person in the scene, which is less likely to happen with taller models.

Additionally, the ability of our model to handle people of various sizes and pedestrians performing unusual actions, such as jumping or bending, are illustrated in Fig. 3.15. Note that, on the first two rows of this figure, the 4-year-old boy, who

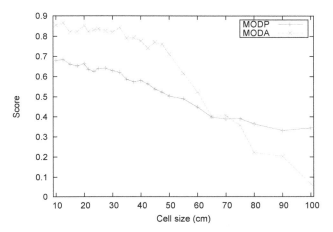

Figure 3.16: Influence of the grid resolution on POM's performance. Detection accuracy (MODA) and precision (MODP) are plotted for different cell sizes. We see that, although precision decreases almost linearly with cell size, accuracy starts dropping for sizes larger than 35 cm.

measures approximately half of an adult height, is correctly detected. His sister, who is smaller than 80 cm, does not appear on the detection maps.

Grid Resolution As discussed in Chapter 2.2, the grid resolution plays an important role in POM's performance. When fine, POM converges normally, because for every possible foreground blob, there exists a corresponding grid location that reasonably fits. However, a fine resolution also comes with a higher computational complexity, as illustrated by Fig. 3.26. On the other hand, if the grid resolution is coarse, there are real-world locations that are badly explained by grid positions, which results in bad convergence from POM and eventually missed detections. The influence of the grid resolution on POM general performance is illustrated by Fig. 3.16, which plots POM's detection precision and accuracy evaluated on the *laboratory* sequence, for different grid sizes. Given that a pedestrian occupies a space roughly approximated by a cylinder of 50 cm diameter, those numbers make sense. The precision decreases linearly when the location size increases, because the fit between the rectangle projection and the real foreground blobs gets worse with rougher grid resolution. On the other hand, the accuracy is stable for grid locations smaller than 35cm, then starts decreasing and drops even faster when this size exceeds 45 cm. Beyond the critical location size of 35 cm, blobs located in the middle of adjacent locations do not fit any of them properly, and missed detections start to appear.

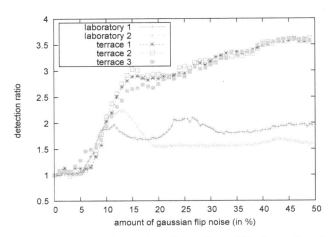

Figure 3.17: Influence of noise on the number of detections. This figure plots the ratio between the number of detections for noise-free frames and frames with independent flip noise. The curves correspond to different sequences from both the *laboratory* and *terrace* data sets.

Input Noise   The quality of background subtraction also affects significantly the detector's performance. First, moving objects in the background, such as tree foliage or cars passing by, act as noise on background subtraction and can disrupt the correct detection process. To try to characterize this phenomenon, we randomly selected 100 frames in 5 sequences from the *laboratory* and *terrace* data set. For each of these frames, we first performed normal detection, and the number of detections thus obtained was used as reference. We then added an increasing amount of independent flip noise on the background masks, at pixel level, and applied POM on the noisy images. Fig. 3.20 shows the effect of the noise on a background subtraction image. On Fig. 3.17, we plot the ratio of detections compared to the original noise-free image. Here we just look at the number of detections, regardless of whether they are true or false positives. This allows to run the test also on sequences for which we do not have a ground truth. Interestingly, we notice that the performance is not affected by an amount of noise up to 5%. Beyond this value, the noise clearly starts altering the results.

To quantify even more precisely the background noise influence, we added various amounts of independent flip noise on the binary images of two video sequences for which we have the ground truth, and evaluated their precision and accuracy results. The results are shown on Fig. 3.18 and confirm those of Fig. 3.17: the detector is almost not affected by up to 5% of background noise, but performance drops rapidly when this value is exceeded. Fig. 3.19 plots the same results in terms of true and false positive rates, and shows that both rates are affected by an increase of background noise.

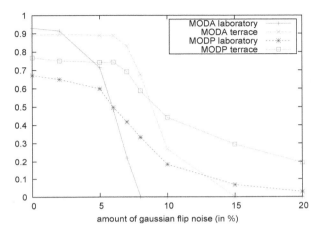

Figure 3.18: Influence of background noise on POM's performance. Various amounts of independent flip noise have been added to two video sequences from the *laboratory* data set, and the *terrace* data set respectively. The detection precision (MODP) and accuracy (MODA) metrics applied to the noisy results are plotted.

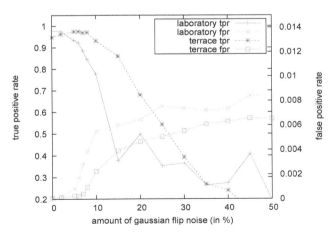

Figure 3.19: Influence of background noise on POM's performance. Various amounts of independent flip noise have been added to two video sequences from the *laboratory* data set, and the *terrace* data set respectively. POM results are evaluated in terms of true and false positive rates.

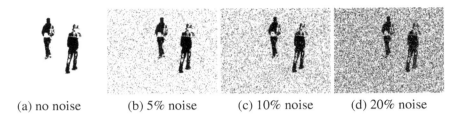

(a) no noise   (b) 5% noise   (c) 10% noise   (d) 20% noise

Figure 3.20: Illustration of the amounts of flip noise added to generate Figs. 3.17, 3.18 and 3.19.

Another important factor potentially altering the performance of the detector is the quality of the binary blobs produced by background subtraction. Our generative model makes a very rough approximation of the foreground blobs by a rectangle, which implies that the detector is hardly affected by the general shapes of the blobs. However, the ratio of detected pixels in a silhouette is important for the convergence of our algorithm. To quantify this relation, we have again added noise to the same two labelled sequences. This time, however, we added subtractive noise, instead of flip noise, which slowly erased the foreground blobs without affecting the rest of the image. The evaluation of this process with the MODP and MODA metrics is plotted in Fig. 3.21. The difference with Fig. 3.18 is striking: POM is very resistant to uniform alterations of the foreground blobs. Amounts of noise up to 60% only slightly affect the overall performance, and detection quality only really decreases beyond 80%. The same results are plotted in terms of true and false positives in Fig. 3.22. Logically, only the true positive rate is affected by the foreground blobs deterioration. Again the effects of the noise are shown on Fig. 3.23.

Determining σ The parameter σ introduced in Eq. 3.3, accounts for the quality of the background subtraction, in the pseudo-distance function Ψ between a background subtraction image B^c and an ideal image A^c. This is the only parameter that needs to be tuned in the POM detector. Empirically, we have found that a value of 0.01 gives the best results in almost all situations. Figure 3.24 illustrates this fact experimentally, by plotting detection precision and accuracy as a function of σ. As can be seen, the optimal value is very close to 0.01.

Number of Cameras   Finally, the last important variable in the detection process is the number of cameras. Most of the sequences in our database have been acquired by 4 cameras. The reason was essentially the availability of the video material, and the fact that 4 cameras allow a decent and even coverage of a scene without any blind spot. Of course, the number of necessary cameras for a good detection also strongly depends on the expected density of the crowd monitored. While it never hurts, in terms of detection performance, to have additional cameras, it also introduces a non

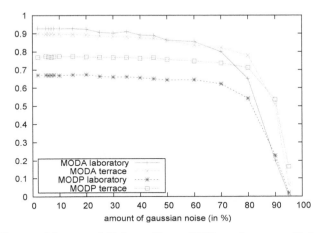

Figure 3.21: Influence of foreground blobs quality on POM's performance. Various amounts of Gaussian noise were subtracted from the foreground blobs of two video sequences from the *laboratory* and the *terrace* data sets. The detection precision (MODP) and accuracy (MODA) metrics applied to the noisy results are plotted.

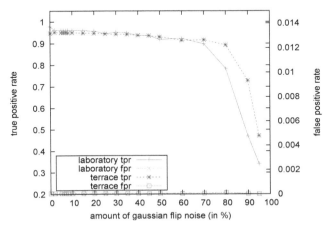

Figure 3.22: Influence of foreground blobs quality on POM's performance. Various amounts of Gaussian noise were subtracted from the foreground blobs of two video sequences from the *laboratory* and the *terrace* data sets. POM results are evaluated in terms of true and false positive rates.

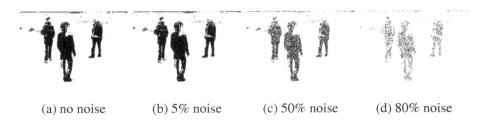

(a) no noise   (b) 5% noise   (c) 50% noise   (d) 80% noise

Figure 3.23: Illustration of the amounts of subtractive noise added to generate Figs. 3.21 and 3.22.

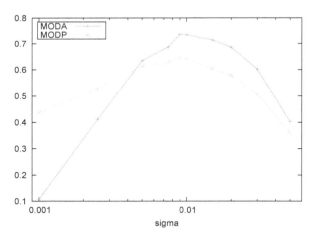

Figure 3.24: Influence of the parameter σ on POM's performance, measured on the PETS sequence. The detection precision (MODP) and accuracy (MODA) metrics are used for evaluation. A value of 10^{-2} gives the best performance empirically, and is used in almost all our experiments.

negligible computational cost. Therefore, for any given environment, there is an ideal number of cameras, beyond which the detection performance no longer improves.

To generate a more quantitative picture of this phenomenon, we have run our detection algorithm on three of our sequences with various numbers of cameras, from the initial configuration down to the monocular case. Each of the detection results has been evaluated using the usual CLEAR metrics and the result is plotted on Fig. 3.25. At first glance, we see that the accuracy (MODA) is generally more affected than the precision (MODP), which means that the diminution of camera views essentially translates into an increase of miss-detections and false positives. Interestingly, varying the number of views does not affect equally all the sequences. In both the *laboratory* and *terrace*, the performance is quite stable for 3 cameras and drops faster for 2 and 1 camera. On the other hand, the PETS sequence is relatively unaltered by the reduction in the number of cameras. The origin of this difference stems from the different camera setups used in these environments. In both the *laboratory* and the *terrace* sequences, the cameras are located quite low on the ground, at about the same height as people's heads, thus generating numerous occlusions. For occlusion handling, the use of several cameras with different viewpoints is crucial, thus the strong relation between the number of cameras and the algorithm's performance. For the PETS sequence, half of the cameras were located about two meters above the ground, while the other half were fixed higher, around 6 meters above the ground. The amount of occlusions occurring on those cameras is thus relatively low. Moreover, the camera #1 - i.e. the one that is used in the monocular case - gives a very clear view on almost the whole monitored area, as can be seen in Fig. 3.14. It is therefore not surprising that the performance does not decrease much as we drop cameras. A careful look can even see that performance improves when going from 6 to 5 cameras and from 2 to 1. The reason is that some cameras were badly calibrated, and ignoring them can be beneficial for the detection quality. Monocular detection results on the PETS sequence are shown in Fig. 3.14.

3.2.6.2 Run Time

The last remaining aspect of the evaluation is the algorithm's speed. To be useful in the widest number of applications, a detection algorithm needs to run close to real-time. Thanks to its design based on integral images, the POM algorithm is able to perform people detection very quickly, as illustrated in Fig. 3.26. To generate the corresponding graph, we have run POM on 100 consecutive frames of a video sequence part of the *laboratory* data set. Plotted is the average run time for one detection, with various grid and image sizes. Obviously, the complexity is linear with respect to grid size. Also, downsampling the input image results in a significant speed gain, while barely affecting the algorithms performance: hardly any information is lost while downsampling binary blobs. Note that for images of 90×72 and grid sizes of up to

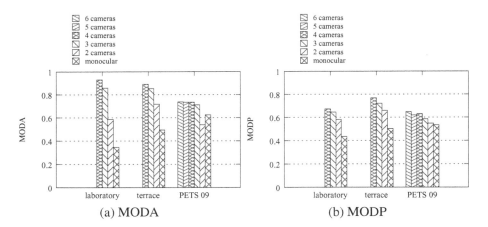

(a) MODA   (b) MODP

Figure 3.25: Influence of the number of cameras on POM's performance. Three test sequences from the *laboratory*, *terrace* and PETS data sets have been processed using a decreasing number of camera views. The left graph plots the accuracy (MODA) results, while the right one plots the precision (MODP) ones.

1,500 locations, the detection process is taking less than 40 ms, which means that it could run in real-time on 25 fps video sequences. Of course, these numbers include the detection process only, and the time for background subtraction and other image transmission should be added to determine the speed of a complete detection system.

Sparse grids   To reduce the algorithm complexity, one can use sparse grids [1]. The idea is fairly simple: Instead of using the whole ground plane grid, one can eliminate all grid locations whose rectangle projections in the camera views are not substantially intersecting the foreground blobs. Only the retained locations are then used during POM optimization. Of course, the sparse grid needs to be recomputed at every new input image. By so doing, the actual grid size used for computation can be usually reduced more than 10 times, without any decrease in detection quality. The benefit is a lower complexity, and a weaker dependency on grid size. Fig. 3.27 compares the runtime when using sparse grids with the one achieved on full grids. For the same parameters, the speed gain is between 2 and 3 times. Additionally, one can notice that the curves are flatter, characteristic of a weaker dependency on grid size.

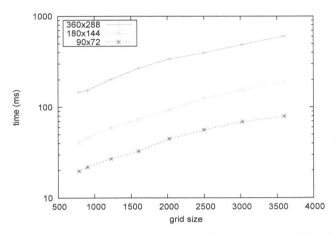

Figure 3.26: POM's runtime for various grid sizes and input image dimensions. Note that the y axis is in log scale. This runtime includes only POM's iterative algorithm and not the background subtraction procedure.

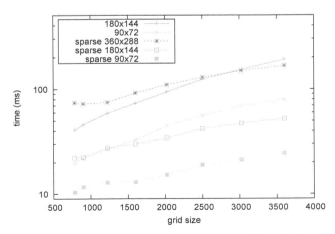

Figure 3.27: Comparison of POM runtime using sparse grids versus full grids. For the same parameters a speed gain between 2 and 3 times can be observed.

3.2.7   Discussion

The quality of the occupancy map estimation can be affected by three sources of errors: The poor quality of the output of the background subtraction, the presence of people in an area covered by only one camera, and the excessive proximity of several individuals.

In practice, the first two difficulties only result in actual errors when they occur simultaneously, which is relatively rare and could be made even rarer by using a more sophisticated approach to background subtraction: The main weakness of the methods we currently use is that they may produce blobs that are too large due to reflections on walls or glossy floors. This does not affect performance if an individual is seen in multiple views but may make him appear to be closer than he truly is, if seen in a single view. Similarly, shadows are segmented as moving parts and can either make actual silhouettes appear larger or create ghosts.

The third difficulty is more serious and represents the true limitation of our approach. When there are too many people in the scene for any background subtraction algorithm to resolve them as individual blobs in at least one view, the algorithm will fail to correctly detect and locate all the individuals. The largest number of people that we can currently handle is hard to quantify because it depends on the scene configuration, the number of cameras, and their exact locations. However, some results presented in this section are close to the upper limit our algorithm can tolerate with the specific camera configurations we use. A potential solution to this problem would be to replace background subtraction by part-based people detectors that could still respond in a crowd.

Despite its effectiveness at pedestrian detection, the Probabilistic Occupancy Map approach suffers from another limitation shared by many methods relying on background subtraction: It is not able to discriminate pedestrians from other moving objects. A restricting assumption needed for POM to work correctly is thus that only pedestrians are moving in front of the cameras. Small objects, such as a ball, would not be a problem, because they would be ignored due to their small size. However, object of roughly the same size as people would be detected as pedestrians. Larger objects might also be detected as a group of people.

In the second part of this chapter, we therefore study a slightly different approach to people detection from multiple views, which replaces the initial background subtraction stage by an independent monocular pedestrian detection, and then merges the results on individual views by taking into account a learnt response model of the pedestrian detector. The main benefit of this approach over POM is the ability to focus only on pedestrians and ignore other moving objects.

3.3 Detection by Classification

Here we propose a second approach to people detection from multiple views. Compared to POM, this new approach replaces the initial background subtraction stage by image-based detection with a classifier trained at recognizing pedestrians. Our motivation is to be able to distinguish pedestrians from other object motions, which background subtraction cannot do.

In this application, a classifier is repeatedly applied to every possible 3-D pose in different camera views, which results in one map of classifier answers per camera view. The several maps of classifier answers are then post-processed and combined by our algorithm to yield the final detection.

At the heart of our approach is a sophisticated application of Bayes' law. Using a model of the responses of a classifier given the true occupancy, we infer a posterior probability on the occupancy given the classifier responses. We will show that this lets us combine the multiple and noisy classifier responses in separate camera views and infer accurate world coordinates for our detections.

Few other approaches have attempted to combine the output of detectors across views to overcome the problems created by occlusions in a principled way. In [64], the algorithm classifies individual pixels as background or part of a moving object and combines these results across views by assuming independence given the presence of a pedestrian at a certain ground location. Hence, this scheme does not use a generic pedestrian detector based on a high-level model of silhouettes and textures. Neither does it explicitly model the fact that a detection in one view is influenced by the presence of distant pedestrians creating occlusions, which, as we will see, can trigger many false alarms. By contrast, the M_2Tracker [87] explicitly models the relation between multiple pedestrians and the image at the pixel level, thus naturally taking occlusions into account. However, this approach relies on temporal consistency, and since it is based on a tight integration between the handling of occlusions and a color-based appearance model, it cannot be generalized to use a generic pedestrian vs. background classifier.

In contrast to the approaches described above, our method relies on classifiers applied on separate views independently. We explicitly integrate occlusion effects between locations and quantitative knowledge about the classifier invariance to pose change into a sound Bayesian framework to combine the multiple classifier answers and yield the final detection.

3.3.1 Overview

We start by giving an overview of our algorithm, before going into more details in the following subsections. We use notations summarized in Table 3.3.

We keep the occupancy grid formalism introduced in Chapter 2.2. In our setup,

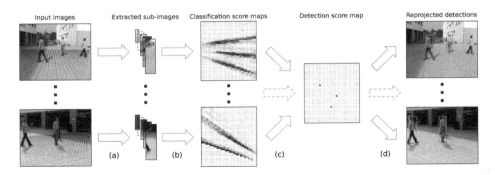

Figure 3.28: Overview of the detection process. Video sequences are acquired by widely separated and calibrated cameras. The ground plane of the tracked area is discretized into a finite number of locations, depicted by the black dots in the leftmost column. (a) We first extract from each image the rectangular sub-images that correspond to the average height of a person at each of these locations. (b) We apply a classifier trained to recognize pedestrians to each sub-image to estimate probabilities of occupancy in the ground plane from each view *independently*. (c) We use the algorithm that is at the core of this paper to combine the individual classification score maps into a single detection score map. (d) We re-project into the original images a person-sized rectangle located at local maxima of the probability estimate.

an area of interest is filmed by C widely separated and calibrated cameras. We discretize the ground plane into a regular grid of K locations separated by 25cm, and use rectangular shapes defined in Chapter 2.3 to link the top and camera views together. This way, we can determine, for every camera view c and every location k, the sub-image $\mathcal{I}_k^c = I^c \otimes \mathcal{A}_k^c$, whose dimension roughly corresponds to the average size of a person that would be standing at location k (see Fig. 3.2, page 42 for some examples). Our algorithm involves two main steps:

1. For each camera c and ground plane location k, the algorithm extracts sub-image $\mathcal{I}_k^c$. Classifiers based on decision trees are then applied to every sub-image $\mathcal{I}_k^c$, as shown on Fig. 3.29. These classifiers have been trained at recognizing pedestrians, and their answer on sub-image $\mathcal{I}_k^c$ can be interpreted as a rough probability of occupancy of ground plane location k, given the sub-image. This first step thus produces as many *classification score maps* (see third column of Fig. 3.28) as there are cameras and is described in §3.3.2.

2. The several classification score maps, generated during step 1, are now combined into a final probability of occupancy map (called hereafter *detection score map*), such as the one of the fourth column of Fig. 3.28. This represents an estimate of $P(X^k = 1 \,|\, I^1, \ldots, I^C)$, the true marginal of the probabilities of presence at every location, given the full signal.

We compare two approaches for the second step. Section §3.3.3 describes the

Table 3.3: Notation

C	number of cameras.
K	number of locations in the ground plane ($\simeq 1000$).
X^k	Boolean random variable standing for the occupancy of location k on the ground plane.
I^c	input image from camera c.
$\mathscr{I}_k^c$	rectangular human size sub-window cropped from camera view c at ground location k.
$\delta^c(i,j)$	horizontal distance between the centers of $\mathscr{I}_i^c$ and $\mathscr{I}_j^c$ on camera view c.
n_k^c	neighborhood of k on camera c, $\left\{ j \neq k, \mathscr{I}_j^c \cap \mathscr{I}_k^c \neq \emptyset \right\}$.
T_k^c	sum of the responses of the binary decision trees at ground location k in camera view c, thus an integer value in $\{0, ..., N_T\}$ where N_T is the number of decision trees.
$\mathbf{T}$	vector of all the T_k^c.
R	the product law with the same marginals as the real posterior distribution $P(\cdot \mid \mathbf{T})$. $R(\mathbf{X}) = \prod_{k=1}^K R(X^k)$.
E_R	expectation under $\mathbf{X} \sim R$. $E_R(x) = \int xR(x)dx$.
r_k	the marginal probability of R, i.e. $R(X^k = 1)$.
$\|.\|$	area of a sub-image.

one, which is representative of what is usually performed by state-of-the-art methods. We refer to it as the *baseline* because it combines the individual classification score maps without taking into account the interactions between the presence of pedestrian due to occlusion. By contrast, the second approach takes into account potential occlusions and knowledge about the classifier behavior and yields a substantial increase in performance. It is at the core of our contribution and is discussed in §3.3.4.

3.3.2 Classification Score Maps

We introduce the classifier we use for single-view pedestrian detection and to compute our classification score maps.

3.3.2.1 Classifier as a Pedestrian Detector

During a learning step, we create a set of decision trees dedicated to the classification of rectangular images into two classes: "person" or "background". The binary decision trees we use as classifiers are based on thresholded Haar wavelets operating

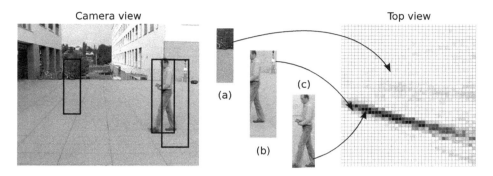

Figure 3.29: Generation of the *classification score maps*. Images (a), (b) and (c) show sub-windows extracted from the camera view at 3 random locations of the ground plane. Classifiers are applied to sub-images $\mathscr{I}_k^c$ corresponding to every ground plane location k. Images depicting background (a) produce a low classification score for the corresponding location. Images showing badly centered pedestrian (b) produce a slightly higher score and images featuring a well centered pedestrian (c) receive high score.

on grayscale images [126], illustrated by Fig. 3.30. They are trained using a few thousands of images of different sizes, each of which represents either a pedestrian correctly centered in the rectangular frame, or *background*, which could be anything else.

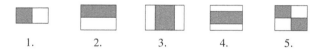

Figure 3.30: The five types of rectangle features used by the decision trees.

More specifically, for every tree, several hundreds of features of different scales, orientations and aspect ratios are generated randomly and applied to our training set. The one that best separates the two populations according to Shanon's entropy is kept as the root node and the training set is split and then dropped into two similarly-constructed sub-nodes [16]. This process is repeated until either the *person* and *background* sets are completely separated or it reaches the tree maximum depth $d = 5$. Typical features picked by a decision tree are displayed on Fig. 3.31. Our classifier consists of a forest [15] of $N_T = 31$ decision trees built in this manner.

3.3.2.2 Computing Classification Score Maps

At runtime, the algorithm iterates through every camera and ground location, extracts a sub-image corresponding to the rectangular shape of human size, and takes its score to be the number of trees classifying the sub-image as "person" (Fig. 3.29).

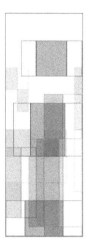

Figure 3.31: Example of features selected by one decision tree. Colors are used to separate different feature types.

If we see the individual tree responses as many i.i.d. samples of the response of an ideal classifier, the classification score in location k is an estimate of the probability for such a classifier to respond that k is actually occupied given the sub-image at that location. Hence, it is a good indicator of the actual occupancy.

This stage produces, for each camera, a map such as the ones depicted by the third column of Fig. 3.28 or by the three left pictures in Fig. 3.32, which assigns a voting score to every ground location. As shown on those figures, detected pedestrians appear as "cone shapes" in the axis of the camera, on the classification score maps. This is due to the high invariance in scale and the limited invariance in translation of the classifiers, and hinders precise people location. Hence the need of an extra

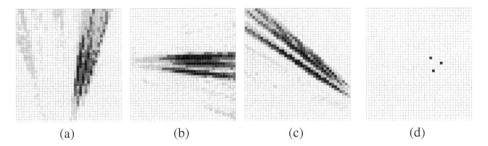

(a)	(b)	(c)	(d)

Figure 3.32: Images (a), (b) and (c) show the *classification score maps* of a scene viewed under three different angles. Image (d) represents the corresponding ground truth.

step, which combines classification score maps from different camera views into one accurate detection score map. Sections §3.3.3 and §3.3.4 present two possible methods for this operation.

3.3.3   Baseline Approach

The *baseline approach* consists of multiplying the responses of the trees from different viewpoints. This is essentially what the product rule used in [64] does. It is more sophisticated than a crude clustering and averaging in separated views, since it assumes the conditional independence between the different views, given the true occupancy. Recall that T_k^c is an integer standing for the sum of the trees' answers at location k on camera view c, and $\mathbf{T}$ is the vector of all T_k^c. Formally, we have

$$P(X^k = \alpha \,|\, \mathbf{T}) \;=\; P(X^k = \alpha \,|\, T_k^1, \ldots, T_k^C) \qquad (3.29)$$

$$= \frac{P(X^k = \alpha)}{P(T_k^1, \ldots, T_k^C)} P(T_k^1, \ldots, T_k^C \,|\, X^k = \alpha) \qquad (3.30)$$

$$= \frac{P(X^k = \alpha)}{P(T_k^1, \ldots, T_k^C)} \prod_c P(T_k^c \,|\, X^k = \alpha). \qquad (3.31)$$

Equality (3.29) is true under the assumption that only the responses of the trees at location k bring information about the occupancy at that location, equality (3.30) is directly Bayes' law, and equality (3.31) is true under the assumption that given the occupancy of location k, the trees' responses at that location from different camera views are independent.

We then model the probability of the trees' response at a certain point given that it is occupied ($\alpha = 1$) by a density proportional to the number of trees responding at that point, and the probability of response when the location is empty ($\alpha = 0$) by a constant response. This leads to a final rule that multiplies the responses of the trees from the different viewpoints to estimate a score increasing with the probability of occupancy at that point.

3.3.4   Principled Approach

The baseline method of the previous section assumes that, given the true occupancy at a certain location, the responses of the trees at that point for different viewpoints are independent from each other, and are not influenced by occupancy at other locations. As shown in Section §3.3.5, it usually triggers many false alarms. By contrast, our principled approach relies on an assumption of conditional independence of the tree responses at any location k, given the occupancy of the full grid $(X^1, \ldots, X^K)$, and not anymore X^k alone. Such an assumption is far more realistic, and leads to an algorithm which takes into account the long-range influence of both the occlusions between pedestrians and the presence of an individual on the classification score maps, due to the invariance of the classifiers.

3.3.4.1 Conditional Marginals

We want to compute numerically, at every location k of the ground plane, $P(X^k | \mathbf{T})$ the conditional marginal probability of presence given the response of the classifiers at all locations. We will show that computing this quantity requires $P(\mathbf{T} | \mathbf{X})$, the tree response model given the ground occupancy. It is learnt by applying the classifier on sequences for which we have a ground truth, and is described in §3.3.4.2. As explained below, there is no possible analytical way to obtain $P(X^k | \mathbf{T})$ given our underlying assumptions, hence the need to evaluate it numerically through an iterative process. At each new iteration, the marginal probabilities of presence $P(X^k | \mathbf{T})$ for all ground locations k are reevaluated using their previous estimate, until convergence.

Let $\mathbf{X}^{j \neq k}$ denote the vector $(X^1, \ldots, X^{k-1}, X^{k+1}, \ldots, X^K)$, R the product law with the same marginals as the posterior $\forall k$, $R(X^k = 1) = P(X^k = 1 | \mathbf{T})$ and E_R the expectation under $\mathbf{X} \sim R$, as summarized in Table 3.3. To obtain a tractable form for $r_k^\alpha = P(X^k = \alpha | \mathbf{T})$, we first marginalize $\mathbf{X}^{j \neq k}$

$$
\begin{aligned}
r_k^\alpha &= \sum_{\mathbf{X}^{j \neq k}} P(X^k = \alpha | \mathbf{T}, \mathbf{X}^{j \neq k}) P(\mathbf{X}^{j \neq k} | \mathbf{T}) \\
&= E[P(X^k = \alpha | \mathbf{T}, \mathbf{X}^{j \neq k}) | \mathbf{T}],
\end{aligned}
\tag{3.32}
$$

where $\mathbf{T}$ is equal to the observed trees' answers and the only random quantity in the expectation is $\mathbf{X}$. We then apply Bayes' law to make the model of the trees' answers given the true occupancy state appear

$$
r_k^\alpha = E\left[\frac{P(\mathbf{T} | X^k = \alpha, \mathbf{X}^{j \neq k}) P(X^k = \alpha, \mathbf{X}^{j \neq k})}{P(\mathbf{X}^{j \neq k} | \mathbf{T}) P(\mathbf{T})} \middle| \mathbf{T} \right].
\tag{3.33}
$$

However, there is no analytical expression for (3.33), and we thus have to estimate the expectation numerically by sampling the $\mathbf{X}^{j \neq k}$ and averaging the corresponding probability. To this end, we substitute the expectation under the true posterior law by a re-weighted expectation under a product law R with the conditional marginals as marginal

$$
\begin{aligned}
r_k^\alpha &= E_R\left[\frac{P(\mathbf{T} | X^k = \alpha, \mathbf{X}^{j \neq k}) P(X^k = \alpha, \mathbf{X}^{j \neq k})}{P(\mathbf{X}^{j \neq k} | \mathbf{T}) P(\mathbf{T})} \frac{P(\mathbf{X}^{j \neq k} | \mathbf{T})}{R(\mathbf{X}^{j \neq k})} \right] \\
&= E_R\left[\frac{P(\mathbf{T} | X^k = \alpha, \mathbf{X}^{j \neq k})}{P(\mathbf{T})} \frac{P(X^k = \alpha, \mathbf{X}^{j \neq k})}{R(\mathbf{X}^{j \neq k})} \right].
\end{aligned}
\tag{3.34}
$$

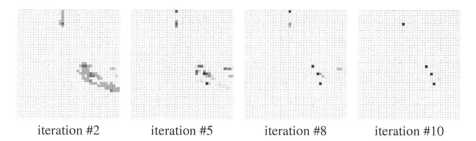

iteration #2   iteration #5   iteration #8   iteration #10

Figure 3.33: Example of convergence of a detection score map during the iterative estimation.

Note that this represents a typical case of importance sampling. Such a formulation ensures that, when we estimate the expectation numerically, the sampling of $\mathbf{X}^{j\neq k}$ will accumulate on the occupancy configurations consistent with the tree responses, thus leading to a far better estimate of the averaging with a reasonable number of samples. Finally we simplify the expression by assuming that the prior distribution is a product law (i.e. $P(\mathbf{X}) = \prod_{k=1}^{K} P(X^k)$)

$$ r_k^\alpha = \frac{P(X^k=\alpha)}{P(\mathbf{T})} E_R\left[P(\mathbf{T}|X^k=\alpha, \mathbf{X}^{j\neq k}) \prod_{j\neq k} \frac{P(X^j)}{R(X^j)} \right]. \qquad (3.35) $$

We end up with an expression of each marginal as a function of the other marginals, thus a large system of equations to solve.

This result is intuitive: the conditional marginal probability of presence at location k given the trees' answers can be computed by fixing X^k, sampling all the other X^j according to the current estimate of R, and averaging the corresponding probability that the trees respond what they actually respond. The more the value associated to X^k makes the actual tree responses likely, the highest its probability.

We get rid of the unknown $P(\mathbf{T})$ quantity by computing

$$ P(X^k=1|\mathbf{T}) = \frac{P(\mathbf{T})P(X^k=1|\mathbf{T})}{P(\mathbf{T})P(X^k=0|\mathbf{T}) + P(\mathbf{T})P(X^k=1|\mathbf{T})}. \qquad (3.36) $$

In the end, we obtain a large number of equations relating the $P(X^k=1|\mathbf{T})$. We can iterate these equations to estimate the conditional marginals. After initialization of all r_ks to a prior value, each of these equations can be evaluated numerically by sampling according to a product law R with the current estimates as marginals. Experimental results show that with such a choice, since the sampling accumulates on the configurations consistent with the observations, a few tens of iterations are sufficient to provide good numerical precision. Fig. 3.33 shows four iterations of the detection score map convergence process.

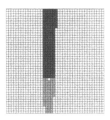

Figure 3.34: Left image shows the neighborhood n_k^c in camera view and right image shows it in top view.

3.3.4.2   Tree Response Model

At the core of Equation (3.35) above is $P(\mathbf{T}\,|\,\mathbf{X})$, the responses of the trees given the true occupancy state, where $\mathbf{X} = (X^1,\dots,X^K)$. It must account for effects such as occlusion and classifier invariance. Assuming that the trees' responses are independent given the true state, we write

$$P(\mathbf{T}\,|\,\mathbf{X}) = \prod_{c,k} P(T_k^c\,|\,\mathbf{X}). \tag{3.37}$$

As shown in Fig. 3.34, the trees' response at position k can only be influenced by ground location j, whose corresponding sub-image $\mathscr{I}_j^c$ intersects the $\mathscr{I}_k^c$. We call such locations the *neighborhood* n_k^c of k on camera view c. Thus, Equation (3.37) becomes

$$P(\mathbf{T}\,|\,\mathbf{X}) = \prod_{c,k} P(T_k^c\,|\,X^k, \mathbf{X}^{n_k^c}), \tag{3.38}$$

where we simply ignore positions outside n_k^c. The classifier response at location k can thus be interpreted as a function of the presence of individuals in the neighborhood of k, as opposed to the whole scene.

In the rest of the section, we show how to express (3.38) numerically in some simple particular cases, and we then extend it to the general case, thus deriving a model for the classifier response.

Empty neighborhood   If the neighborhood of k is empty (Fig. 3.36, (a) and (b)), the trees' answer in k depends only on the occupancy of k. Precisely $\forall \alpha \in \{0,1\}$:

$$P(T_k^c = t\,|\,X^k = \alpha, \forall j \in n_k^c, X^j = 0) = \mu_\alpha(t). \tag{3.39}$$

The functionals μ_0 and μ_1 are modeled as histograms estimated on training samples, and shown on Fig. 3.35(a).

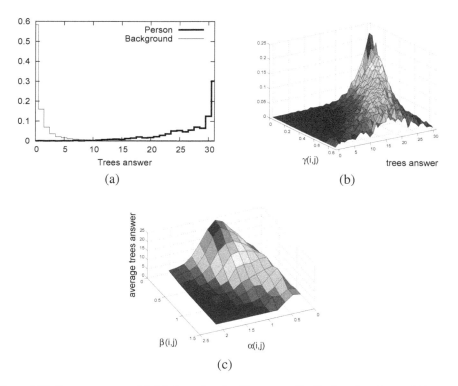

Figure 3.35: Tree response model. (a) shows the classifier answer distributions for a forest of 31 trees, (b) plots the distribution of the classifier answer as a function of $\gamma(i, j)$ and (c) displays the average trees' answer as a function of $\alpha(i, j)$ and $\beta(i, j)$.

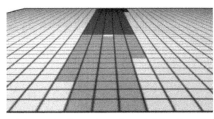

(a) empty location & neighborhood

(b) location occupied, empty *visible* neighborhood

(c) empty location, occupied neighborhood

(d) location & *visible* neighborhood occupied

Figure 3.36: The images above illustrate the four cases used by the tree response model for the grid position k, colored in white. Grid positions highlighted in gray represent the neighborhood n_k^c of position k (see also Fig. 3.34 right, for a top view). The *visible* neighborhood n_k^{c+} is shown in light gray, whereas the neighborhood n_k^{c-} located beyond position k is painted in dark gray. In case (a), neither location k nor its neighborhood is occupied. In case (b), location k is occupied, but its *visible* neighborhood n_k^{c+} is empty. Note that there might or might not be people in n_k^{c-}. In case (c), location k is empty, but there is at least one person in its neighborhood n_k^c. Finally in case (d), location k is occupied, as well as at least one of the locations in n_k^{c+}. As in case (b), it does not matter whether n_k^{c-} is occupied.

One individual in the neighborhood   We now consider the case where only one person is present in the neighborhood of k, at location j. If location k is empty, sub-image $\mathscr{I}_k^c$ will contain some body parts of the person present at location j, in addition to background. This influences the classifier answer in k, in a way that depends on the "distance" between $\mathscr{I}_k^c$ and $\mathscr{I}_j^c$ in the image.

To characterize this pseudo-distance between sub-images, we define functions

$$\alpha(i,j) \;=\; \sqrt{\frac{\|\mathscr{I}_k^c\|}{\|\mathscr{I}_j^c\|}}, \quad \text{and} \tag{3.40}$$

$$\beta(i,j) \;=\; \frac{\delta^c(i,j)}{\sqrt{\|\mathscr{I}_k^c\|}}, \tag{3.41}$$

where $\alpha(i,j)$ quantifies the size ratio between $\mathscr{I}_k^c$ and $\mathscr{I}_j^c$, and $\beta(i,j)$ their misalignment. $\delta^c(i,j)$ is described in Table 3.3.

With this, we obtain the tree response model $\mu_0'(t, \alpha(i,j), \beta(i,j))$, which is computed as histograms from the training samples. It is plotted on Fig. 3.35 (c).

We finally model the case where location k is occupied, with one person present in its neighborhood at location j. For this purpose, we have to distinguish positions from the neighborhood located "behind" k – that is, further from the camera than k – and those located closer to it. We denote the former set by n_k^{c-} and the latter by n_k^{c+} and illustrate them geometrically in Fig. 3.36.

When k is occupied, positions from n_k^{c-} do not influence the classifier answer on $\mathscr{I}_k^c$, but positions from n_k^{c+} do. As for the previous case, we define a pseudo-distance function

$$\gamma(i,j) = \frac{\|\mathscr{I}_k^c \cap \mathscr{I}_j^c\|}{\|\mathscr{I}_k^c\|} \cdot \left(1 - \frac{\|\mathscr{I}_k^c \cap \mathscr{I}_j^c\|}{\|\mathscr{I}_j^c\|}\right), \tag{3.42}$$

with respect to the camera view, to characterize the relationship between the relative position of k and j, and the trees' answer.

We then derive the tree response model for this last case as function $\mu_1'(t, \gamma(i,j))$, which is depicted by Fig. 3.35 (b). It is also computed empirically as histograms from the training samples.

Multiple individuals in the neighborhood   It is not trivial to extend the simplified model with at most one person in the neighborhood to the general case, because the number of neighbor locations is of the order of 100, which implies a huge number of occupancy configurations. We therefore simplify our model by assuming that only the occupied location whose sub-window intersects the most $\mathscr{I}_k^c$ will influence the classifier answer in k, on camera view c. We denote by J_k^{c*} the occupied location from the neighborhood of k, whose corresponding sub-window covers the most $\mathscr{I}_k^c$

$$J_k^{c*} = \underset{j \in n_k^c, X^j=1}{\arg\max} \; \|\mathscr{I}_k^c \cap \mathscr{I}_k^c\|. \tag{3.43}$$

This assumption makes the model tractable and has been found to hold empirically. Finally, we obtain as response model when the neighborhood is not empty, whether there is a single individual or several of them:

$$P\left(T_k^c = t \mid X^k = 0, \exists j \in n_k^c, X^j = 1\right) = \mu_0'(t, \alpha(i, J_k^{c*}), \beta(i, J_k^{c*})) \tag{3.44}$$

$$P\left(T_k^c = t \mid X^k = 1, \exists j \in n_k^{c+}, X^j = 1\right) = \mu_1'(t, \gamma(i, J_k^{c*})) \;. \tag{3.45}$$

3.3.5 Results

We tested our approach on the *campus* data set, described in §2.7, consisting of several video sequences filmed by three outdoor cameras with overlapping fields of view. We used a 2 minute sequence to train the system and learn the trees response model of § 3.3.4.2 and the remaining to test it. To demonstrate the generality of the model, we also show results applied to the *laboratory* data set, that was not used for training purposes. Finally, we show that our method yields meaningful results even from single views.

Baseline vs. Principled Approaches   To compare the approaches of § 3.3.3 and § 3.3.4, we randomly selected 100 frames of the outdoor sequences, manually labeled the true pedestrian locations, and compared them to both their outputs.

The result depicted by Fig. 3.37. shows that the principled approach yields much better estimates of the number of people than the baseline approach, which triggers many false positives. When setting the post-processing threshold so that both approaches have about 10% of false negatives, our approach outperforms the baseline one, by producing only about 0.06% of false positives instead of 0.81%. This result is depicted by the ROC curves of Fig. 3.37.b. Since our method relies on a strong model and produces very peaked occupancy probabilities, detection failures cases produce incorrect occupancy maps. This explains the crossing of the ROC curves at very high detection rates.

Indoor and Outdoor Sequences   Figs. 3.38 and 3.39 depict our results in the outdoor *campus* and indoor *laboratory* sequences respectively. In both cases, people are correctly detected in spite of difficulties: In the outdoor images, there are strong shadows, which could create problems for methods based on background subtraction but do not affect our results. The occlusions in the indoor images are very significant

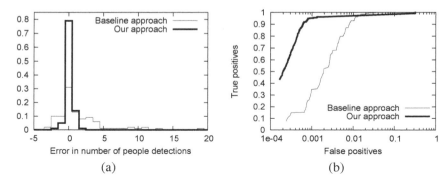

Figure 3.37: Comparing the performance of the baseline and principled approaches. (a) Error distribution in the estimate of the number of people present in the scene. (b) ROC curves for the two methods. These graphs demonstrate that the principled approach truly provides a better estimate of the number of people present in the scene, and a better false positives vs. false negatives ratio.

but are nevertheless handled correctly, especially when one recalls that we do not enforce any form of temporal consistency and treat every time frame independently.

Thanks to the tree response model of Section 3.3.4.2, we can retrieve occupancy maps from the noisy classifier answers, even when using single views as shown in Fig. 3.40. The procedure used is the same as in the multi-view case, except that we do no longer multiply tree's answers from multiple cameras in Equation 3.37. Occlusions are no longer handled, as evidenced by the fact that a half-hidden person in the right image is missed. Nevertheless, the results remain meaningful.

3.3.6 Discussion

The classifier approach to people detection presented above addresses the main issues of the Probabilistic Occupancy Map detector of §3.2, that is its vulnerability to light changes and non-human motion. These weaknesses stem from the background subtraction, which cannot discriminate between different types of motion, and which is inherently sensitive to effects such as light intensity variations, shadows or reflections. By relying on image features, the classifier approach manages to avoid those problems.

However, these benefits comes at a substantial cost: First, the classifiers need training, which involves creating a labelled training set of thousands of pedestrian images. Furthermore, the classifier response model also needs to be learnt, which requires a reference video sequence along with a manually labelled ground truth.

Second, the expectation in Eq. 3.35 can only be estimated by sampling the occupancies X^j according to the product law Q. A similar issue also occurred for

Figure 3.38: Results of our algorithm on the *campus* data set, for which it was trained. Each row shows several views taken at the same time instant from different angles. Boxes are located on local maxima of the estimated probabilities of occupancy. The last column depicts the corresponding detection score map before thresholding.

Figure 3.39: Results of our algorithm on the *laboratory* data set, with classifiers trained on the *campus* one. Each row shows several views taken at the same time instant from different angles. Boxes are located on local maxima of the estimated probabilities of occupancy. The last column depicts the corresponding detection score map before thresholding.

Figure 3.40: Example results on single-view images. Note that occlusions are obviously no longer handled, as evidenced by the fact that a half-hidden person in the right image is missed.

the POM detector in Eq. 3.16, but it was addressed by using the approximation of Eq. 3.17. The consequence of this necessary sampling is a computationally intensive process and slow detections. One can expect up to 10 seconds of processing per frame on a standard computer. This approach is therefore not suited for real-time processing.

Third, despite the large performance gain of our approach compared to a naive method, it still does not perform as good as POM, due to the higher number of false positives it produces. A performance comparison between the 3 approaches is shown on Fig. 3.41. We do not plot the accuracy (MODA) metric, because both classification-based methods generate too many false positives for this metric to be relevant.

In the remainder of this work, we thus rely on the Probabilistic Occupancy Map algorithm to provide the frame-based detections needed by the trackers.

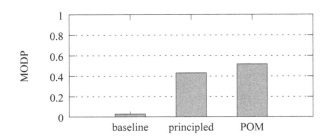

Figure 3.41: Comparison of the two classification-based approaches (baseline and principled) with POM. Results on a *campus* sequence are evaluated with the detection precision (MODP) metric.

Chapter 4

People Tracking

In this chapter, we present two different approaches to linking individual detections provided by a detector at independent time frames. Both approaches are based on global optimization over several consecutive frames, which is more robust than doing it recursively. The general framework used here is still the pedestrian detection using multiple static cameras and an occupancy map, presented in Chapter 2. However, the techniques introduced here are much more generic and can be applied to a wide range of domains, as will be demonstrated. The first method, explained in §4.2, relies on Dynamic Programming [8] applied sequentially on batches of frames to track multiple people. The approach uses the detection maps generated by POM (see §3.2) together with a color model and a motion model. Trajectories are assumed independent and optimized one after the other. In §4.3, we propose another approach to multiple people tracking that formulates the problem as a standard Linear Programming optimization framework. That way multiple trajectories can be jointly optimized. A naive implementation, however, yields a very large problem with many variables and constraints, whose computational complexity is prohibitive. In §4.3.4, we thus introduce a more carefully designed optimization scheme based on the k-shortest paths algorithm [117]. This algorithm takes into account the specificity of our problem and runs in real time.

4.1 State-of-the-Art

Multiple object tracking is an intensively studied area of research. Its primary goal is to generate trajectories of objects by localizing them individually at each frame of a video sequence. This task is usually accomplished by either detecting objects in every frame independently and later linking the detections across frames, or by jointly estimating the objects region and correspondences. Among the methods falling in the later category are those relying on Kernel Tracking [119, 23, 24, 131] or Silhouette Tracking [61, 105]. Kernel Tracking is typically performed by computing the motion of the object, which is represented by a primitive object region, from one frame to the next. The motion is generally in the form of parametric motion or the dense flow field computed in subsequent frames [137]. Silhouette Tracking provides an accurate shape description for objects with complex shapes, such as pedestrians. The goal of a silhouette-based object tracker is to find the object region in each frame by means of an object model generated using the previous frames. This model can be in the form of a color histogram, object edges or the object contour [137]. In this work, we concentrate on the first category of trackers, that is, methods that perform detection and tracking separately. They typically require an external mechanism to detect the objects in every frame. These approaches have the advantage of being resistant to divergence: The detection process can fail on successive frames and still recover at any time because there is no temporal update. Besides, this scheme allows us to use the detector described in the previous chapter. In the following, we thus review state-of-the-art methods for generating tracks by linking detected objects.

Kalman Filter   A large class of approaches relies on the recursive update of tracks with the most recent detections. For instance, Kalman filtering is an efficient way to address multi-target tracking when the number of objects remains small. It is also well suited for real-time applications and has been extensively used in the vision community [14, 87, 58, 134, 77]. However, when the number of objects increases, identity switches become more frequent and are difficult to correct, due to the recursive nature of the method. Moreover, Kalman filter assumes that the state variables are normally distributed, and thus estimates those variables poorly, if the Gaussian assumption does not hold.

Particle Filter   Particle filtering represents the conditional state density by a set of samples and can thus estimate non-Gaussian distributions, which addresses a limitation of Kalman filter. It is often associated with JPDAF or MHT to follow several targets simultaneously [125, 44, 111, 67, 135, 82]. This technique has been used to great effect to follow multiple hockey players [94] or to track multiple people in the ground and image planes simultaneously [31]. In the same spirit, [138] relies on data-driven MCMC to recover trajectories of targets using a batch of observations. [78] applies a Probability Hypothesis Density filter to tracking multiple objects from noisy observations, and therefore falls into this family of algorithms. Despite their success, in our experience, those sampling-based methods typically require careful tuning of several meta-parameters, which reduces the generality of systems that rely on it. Besides, they can only look at small time windows, because their state space grows exponentially with the number of frames.

Hybrid Methods   In an attempt to increase tracking robustness, some methods rely on a dual-stage approach. Detections are first connected into short tracks, which are then linked together using a higher-level method. For example, [99] relies on Kalman filtering to obtain basic tracks, and then tries to merge and split the tracks using the Hungarian algorithm. [54] explores the hierarchical version of the same concept, while [76] uses a variant of AdaBoost to automatically learn the best criterion for linking low-level tracks together. Similarly, [7] turns observations into trajectory segments using local PCA, and then links those segments based on their spatial proximity and smoothness constraints. [42] relies on mean-shift or particle filtering to generate tracklets from detection results. In a second stage, they use MCMC data association to combine the tracklets into full tracks, and to automatically estimate the best parameters for the model. [36] uses a motion model and nearest neighbor to build tracks out of heads detected from a top mounted calibrated camera. The tracks thus generated are then merged and split into the final trajectories using heuristics based on overlap, direction and speed. [17] proposes another method to tracklet generation in a crowded environment, without however going all the way to combining them into complete tracks. They detect multiple people and create tracklets by applying Bayesian clustering on simple tracked image features. By contrast, [92] concentrates on the high level task. The authors assume that a track graph has already been produced and focus on linking identities in the provided track graph. They formulate the multi-object tracking as a Bayesian network inference problem and apply this method to tracking multiple soccer players.

While effective, the approaches mentioned above generally concentrate on a small time window and do not look for a joint global optimum among all trajectories. They are therefore prone to mistakes such as identity switches. To improve robustness to wrong identity assignment, research has recently focused on linking detections over a larger time window using various optimization methods. For example, [65] applies graph cuts to extract trajectories from a batch of people detections obtained using homographic constraints on images from a multi-camera system. [74] simultaneously optimizes detections and tracks, coupled into a Quadratic Boolean Problem and solved by an E-M algorithm.

Greedy Global Optimization Dynamic Programming [8] can be used to link multiple detections over time, and therefore solve the multi-target tracking problem. Moreover, it can be extended to enable the optimization of several trajectories simultaneously [130]. Unfortunately, the computational complexity of such an approach can be prohibitive. While efficient for very small state-space, it does not scale to the size of problems we generally deal with. A different formulation is chosen by [109], where a directed graph, with nodes standing for actual detections, represents the multi-frame point correspondence problem. A greedy optimization algorithm is introduced to efficiently solve the problem, but without a guarantee to find a global optimum.

Linear Programming   Linear Programming is another optimization method that has been applied to find global optima and solve the data association problem on air radar detections [116] or tackle multiple people tracking [59]. Starting from the output of simple object detectors, this last approach builds a network graph in which every node is an observation fully connected to future and past observations, in much the same way as in [109]. Objects hiding each other are modeled by specifying spatial conflicts within nodes. Occlusions are handled by introducing a special node type and arc costs are chosen according to object appearances and a motion model. Additionally, another soft constraint helps ensuring spatial layout consistency. A relatively similar graphical model, with nodes representing detections, is built by [140] for multi-people tracking. The global optimum is searched using a min-cost flow algorithm, which exploits the specific structure of the graph to reach the optimum faster than Linear Programming.

Due to their reduced state-space, these methods are computationally efficient. However, [59] requires *a priori* knowledge of the number of objects to be tracked, which seriously limits its applicability in real life situations. Also, with a state-space only consisting of observations, as opposed to all possible locations, they cannot smoothly interpolate trajectories when there are false negatives. Moreover, the choice of arc costs is ad-hoc and involves many parameters, which have to be tuned for each possible application, reducing the generality of the methods.

4.2   Tracking People using Sequential Dynamic Programming

Here we present a first approach at multi-people tracking from the frame-independent output of a multi-camera people detector, such as those described in Chapter 3. Our goal is to track an *a priori* unknown number of people from a few synchronized video streams taken at head level. In this section, we formulate this problem as one of finding the most probable state of a hidden Markov process given the set of images acquired at each time step, which we will refer to as a *temporal frame*. We then briefly outline the computation of the relevant probabilities using the notations summarized by Tables 4.1 and 4.2.

4.2.1   Computing The Optimal Trajectories

We process the video sequences by batches of $T = 100$ frames, each of which includes C images, and we compute the most likely trajectory for each individual. To achieve consistency over successive batches, we only keep the result on the first ten frames and slide our temporal window. This is illustrated on Fig. 4.1.

Figure 4.1: Video sequences are processed by batch of 100 frames. Only the first 10% of the optimization result is kept, and the rest is discarded. The temporal window is then slid forward and the optimization repeated on the new window.

As described in Chapter 2, the ground plane is discretized into a finite number K of regularly spaced 2–D locations. We introduce a virtual hidden location $\mathcal{H}$ that will be used to model entrances and departures from and into the visible area. As opposed to normal grid locations, $\mathcal{H}$ does not correspond to a physical location. It is however connected to all the grid locations that can act as entrance or exit points. Those are typically the door in a closed room, or the border of the grid in an open space.

For a given batch of frames, let $\mathbf{L}_t = (L_t^1, \ldots, L_t^{N^*})$ be the hidden stochastic processes standing for the locations of individuals, whether visible or not. The number N^* stands for the maximum allowable number of individuals in our world. It is large enough so that conditioning on the number of visible ones does not change the probability of a new individual entering the scene. The L_t^n variables therefore take values in $\{1, \ldots, K, \mathcal{H}\}$.

Given $\mathbf{I}_t = (I_t^1, \ldots, I_t^C)$, the images acquired at time t for $1 \leq t \leq T$, our task is to find the values of $\mathbf{L}_1, \ldots, \mathbf{L}_T$ that maximize

$$P(\mathbf{L}_1, \ldots, \mathbf{L}_T \mid \mathbf{I}_1, \ldots, \mathbf{I}_T). \tag{4.1}$$

As will be discussed in §4.2.3.1, we compute this maximum *a posteriori* in a greedy way, processing one individual at a time, including the hidden ones who can move into the visible scene or not. For each one, the algorithm performs the computation under the constraint that no individual can be at a visible location occupied by an individual already processed.

In theory, this approach could lead to undesirable local minima, for example by connecting the trajectories of two separate people. However this does not happen often because our batches are sufficiently long. To further reduce the chances of this, we process individual trajectories in an order that depends on a reliability score so that the most reliable ones are computed first, thereby reducing the potential for confusion when processing the remaining ones. This order also ensures that if an individual remains in the hidden location, all the other people present in the hidden location will also stay there, and therefore do not need to be processed.

Table 4.1: Notation (deterministic quantities)

$W \times H$	image resolution.
C	number of cameras.
K	number of locations in the ground discretization ($\simeq 1000$).
T	number of frames processed in one batch ($= 100$).
t	frame index.
N^*	virtual number of people, including the non-visible ones.
μ_n^c	color distribution of individual n from camera c.

Our experimental results show that our method does not suffer from the usual weaknesses of greedy algorithms, such as a tendency to get caught in bad local minima. We therefore believe that it compares very favorably to stochastic optimization techniques in general and more specifically particle filtering, which usually requires careful tuning of meta-parameters.

4.2.2 Stochastic Modeling

We will show in §4.2.3.2 that since we process individual trajectories, the whole approach only requires us to define a valid motion model $P(L_{t+1}^n \mid L_t^n = k)$ and a sound appearance model $P(\mathbf{I}_t \mid L_t^n = k)$.

The motion model $P(L_{t+1}^n \mid L_t^n = k)$, which will be introduced in Section §4.2.3.3, is a distribution into a disc of limited radius and center k, which corresponds to a loose bound on the maximum speed of a walking human. Entrance into the scene and departure from it are naturally modeled thanks to the hidden location $\mathcal{H}$, for which we extend the motion model. The probabilities to enter and to leave are similar to the transition probabilities between different ground plane locations.

In Section §4.2.3.4, we will show that the appearance model $P(\mathbf{I}_t \mid L_t^n = k)$ can be decomposed into two terms. The first, described in Section §4.2.3.5, is a very generic color-histogram based model for each individual. The second is the marginal conditional probabilities of occupancy of the ground plane given the results of a background subtraction algorithm, which is the output of the POM algorithm described in Chapter 3.2.

Since these marginal probabilities are computed independently at each time step, they say nothing about identity or correspondence with past frames. The appearance similarity is entirely conveyed by the color histograms, which has experimentally proved sufficient for our purposes.

Table 4.2: Notation (random quantities)

$\mathbf{I}_t$	images from all the cameras $\mathbf{I}_t = (I_t^1, \ldots, I_t^C)$.
$\mathbf{B}_t$	binary images generated by the background subtraction $\mathbf{B}_t = (B_t^1, \ldots, B_t^C)$.
$\mathbf{S}_t$	texture information.
$\mathbf{L}_t$	vector of people locations on the ground plane or in the hidden location $\mathbf{L}_t = (L_t^1, \ldots, L_t^{N^*})$. Each of these random variables takes values into $\{1, \ldots, K, \mathcal{H}\}$, where $\mathcal{H}$ is the hidden place.
$\mathbf{L}^n$	trajectory of individual n, $\mathbf{L}^n = (L_1^n, \ldots, L_T^n)$.
$\mathbf{X}_t$	vectors of boolean random variable $(X_t^1, \ldots, X_t^K)$ standing for the occupancy of location k on the ground plane $(X_t^k = 1) \Leftrightarrow (\exists n, L_t^n = k)$.

4.2.3 Computation of the Trajectories

In Section §4.2.3.1, we break the global optimization of several people's trajectories into the estimation of optimal individual trajectories. In Section §4.2.3.2, we show how this can be performed using the classical Viterbi's algorithm based on dynamic programming. This requires a motion model given in Section §4.2.3.3 and an appearance model described in §4.2.3.4, which combines a color model given in Section §4.2.3.5 and the ground plane occupancy computed by the POM detector.

We use the discrete grid model of Chapter 2.2, in which the visible area is partitioned into a regular grid of K locations as shown in Fig. 2.9, page 26.

4.2.3.1 Multiple Trajectories

Recall that we denote by $\mathbf{L}^n = (L_1^n, \ldots, L_T^n)$ the trajectory of individual n. Given a batch of T temporal frames $\mathbf{I} = (\mathbf{I}_1, \ldots, \mathbf{I}_T)$, we want to maximize the posterior conditional probability

$$P(\mathbf{L}^1 = \mathbf{l}^1, \ldots, \mathbf{L}^{N^*} = \mathbf{l}^{N^*} \mid \mathbf{I})$$
$$= P(\mathbf{L}^1 = \mathbf{l}^1 \mid \mathbf{I}) \prod_{n=2}^{N^*} P(\mathbf{L}^n = \mathbf{l}^n \mid \mathbf{I}, \mathbf{L}^1 = \mathbf{l}^1, \ldots, \mathbf{L}^{n-1} = \mathbf{l}^{n-1}). \quad (4.2)$$

Simultaneous optimization of all the L^is would be intractable. Instead, we optimize one trajectory after the other, which amounts to looking for

$$\hat{\mathbf{l}}^1 \;=\; \arg\max_{l} P(\mathbf{L}^1 = l \,|\, \mathbf{I}), \tag{4.3}$$

$$\hat{\mathbf{l}}^2 \;=\; \arg\max_{l} P(\mathbf{L}^2 = l \,|\, \mathbf{I}, \mathbf{L}^1 = \hat{\mathbf{l}}^1), \tag{4.4}$$

$$\vdots$$

$$\hat{\mathbf{l}}^{N^*} \;=\; \arg\max_{l} P(\mathbf{L}^{N^*} = l \,|\, \mathbf{I}, \mathbf{L}^1 = \hat{\mathbf{l}}^1, \mathbf{L}^2 = \hat{\mathbf{l}}^2, \ldots). \tag{4.5}$$

Note that under our model, conditioning one trajectory given other ones simply means that it will go through no already occupied location. In other words,

$$P(\mathbf{L}^n = l \,|\, \mathbf{I}, \mathbf{L}^1 = \hat{\mathbf{l}}^1, \ldots, \mathbf{L}^{n-1} = \hat{\mathbf{l}}^{n-1}) = P(\mathbf{L}^n = l \,|\, \mathbf{I}, \forall k < n, \forall t, L_t^n \neq \hat{l}_t^k), \tag{4.6}$$

which is $P(\mathbf{L}^n = l \,|\, \mathbf{I})$ with a reduced set of the admissible grid locations.

Such a procedure is recursively correct: If all trajectories estimated up to step n are correct, then the conditioning only improves the estimate of the optimal remaining trajectories. This would suffice if the image-data were informative enough so that locations could be unambiguously associated to individuals. In practice, this is obviously rarely the case. Therefore, this greedy approach to optimization has undesired side effects. For example, due to partly missing localization information for a given trajectory, the algorithm might mistakenly start following another person's trajectory. This is especially likely to happen if the tracked individuals are located close to each other.

To avoid this kind of failure, we process the images by batches of $T = 100$ and first extend the trajectories that have been found with high confidence – as defined below – in the previous batches. We then process the lower confidence ones. As a result, a trajectory which was problematic in the past and is likely to be problematic in the current batch will be optimized last and thus prevented from "stealing" somebody else's location. Furthermore, this approach increases the spatial constraints on such a trajectory when we finally get around to estimating it.

We use as a confidence score the concordance of the estimated trajectories in the previous batches and the localization cue provided by the estimation of POM. More precisely, the score is the number of time frames where the estimated trajectory passes through a local maximum of the estimated probability of occupancy. When POM does not detect a person on a few frames, the score will naturally decrease, indicating a deterioration of the localization information. Since there is a high degree of overlapping between successive batches, the challenging segment of a trajectory – due to failure of the background subtraction or change in illumination for instance – is met in several batches before it actually happens during the ten kept frames. Thus, the heuristic would have ranked the corresponding individual in the last ones to be processed when such problem occurs.

4.2.3.2 Single Trajectory

Let us now consider only the trajectory $\mathbf{L}^n = (L_1^n, \ldots, L_T^n)$ of individual n over T temporal frames. We are looking for the values $(l_1^n, \ldots, l_T^n)$ in the subset of free locations of $\{1, \ldots, K, \mathcal{H}\}$. The initial location l_1^n is either a known visible location if the individual is visible in the first frame of the batch, or $\mathcal{H}$ if he is not. We therefore seek to maximize

$$P(L_1^n = l_1^n, \ldots, L_T^n = l_T^n \mid \mathbf{I}_1, \ldots, \mathbf{I}_T) = \frac{P(\mathbf{I}_1, L_1^n = l_1^n, \ldots, \mathbf{I}_T, L_T^n = l_T^n)}{P(\mathbf{I}_1, \ldots, \mathbf{I}_T)}. \qquad (4.7)$$

Since the denominator is constant with respect to $\mathbf{l}^n$, we simply maximize the numerator, that is, the probability of both the trajectories and the images. Let us introduce the maximum of the probability of both the observations and the trajectory ending up at location k at time t

$$\Phi_t(k) = \max_{l_1^n, \ldots, l_{t-1}^n} P(\mathbf{I}_1, L_1^n = l_1^n, \ldots, \mathbf{I}_t, L_t^n = k). \qquad (4.8)$$

We model jointly the processes L_t^n and $\mathbf{I}_t$ with a hidden Markov model, that is

$$P(L_{t+1}^n \mid L_t^n, L_{t-1}^n, \ldots) = P(L_{t+1}^n \mid L_t^n) \qquad (4.9)$$

and

$$P(I_t, I_{t-1}, \ldots \mid L_t^n, L_{t-1}^n, \ldots) = \prod_t P(I_t \mid L_t^n) \qquad (4.10)$$

Under such a model, we have the classical recursive expression

$$\Phi_t(k) = \underbrace{P(\mathbf{I}_t \mid L_t^n = k)}_{\text{Appearance model}} \max_\tau \underbrace{P(L_t^n = k \mid L_{t-1}^n = \tau)}_{\text{Motion model}} \Phi_{t-1}(\tau) \qquad (4.11)$$

to perform a global search with dynamic programming, which yields the classic Viterbi algorithm. This is straightforward since the L_t^n are in a finite set of cardinality $K+1$.

4.2.3.3 Motion Model

We chose a very simple and unconstrained motion model

$$P(L_t^n = k \mid L_{t-1}^n = \tau) = \begin{cases} 1/Z \cdot e^{-\rho\|k-\tau\|} & \text{if } \|k - \tau\| \leq c \\ 0 & \text{otherwise} \end{cases} \qquad (4.12)$$

where the constant ρ tunes the average human walking speed and c limits the maximum allowable speed. This probability is isotropic, decreases with the distance from location k and is zero for $\|k - \tau\|$ greater than a constant maximum distance. We use a very loose maximum distance c of one square of the grid per frame, which corresponds to a speed of almost 12 mph. We also define explicitly the probabilities of transition to the parts of the scene that are connected to the hidden location $\mathcal{H}$. This is a single door in the *laboratory* or *terrace* sequences and all the contours of the visible area in the *campus* sequence. Thus, entrance and departure of individuals are taken care of naturally by the estimation of the maximum *a posteriori* trajectories. If there are enough evidence from the images that somebody enters or leaves the room, this procedure will estimate that the optimal trajectory does so, and a person will be added to or removed from the visible area.

4.2.3.4 Appearance Model

Recall that our appearance model is given by

$$P(\mathbf{I}_t \,|\, L_t^n = k), \tag{4.13}$$

where $\mathbf{I}_t$ are the input images at time frame t and L_t^n is the random variable representing the location on the grid of individual n, also at time t. From the input images $\mathbf{I}_t$, we use background subtraction to produce binary masks $\mathbf{B}_t$. We denote as $\mathbf{S}_t$ the colors of the pixels inside the blobs and treat the rest of the images as background, which is ignored.

Let X_k^t be a boolean random variable standing for the presence of an individual at location k of the grid at time t. Then we have

$$\overbrace{P(\mathbf{I}_t \,|\, L_t^n = k)}^{\text{Appearance model}} \;=\; \frac{P(\mathbf{I}_t)}{P(L_t^n = k)} P(L_t^n = k \,|\, \mathbf{I}_t) \tag{4.14}$$

$$\propto\; P(L_t^n = k \,|\, \mathbf{I}_t) \tag{4.15}$$

$$=\; P(L_t^n = k \,|\, \mathbf{B}_t, \mathbf{S}_t) \tag{4.16}$$

$$=\; P(L_t^n = k, X_t^k = 1 \,|\, \mathbf{B}_t, \mathbf{S}_t) \tag{4.17}$$

$$=\; P(L_t^n = k \,|\, X_t^k = 1, \mathbf{B}_t, \mathbf{S}_t)\, P(X_t^k = 1 \,|\, \mathbf{B}_t, \mathbf{S}_t)$$

$$=\; \underbrace{P(L_t^n = k \,|\, X_t^k = 1, \mathbf{S}_t)}_{\text{Color model}} \;\; \underbrace{P(X_t^k = 1 \,|\, \mathbf{B}_t)}_{\text{Ground plane occupancy}} \;. \tag{4.18}$$

Equality (4.14) follows directly from Bayes formula. Equality (4.15) is true since the probability of the image – without conditioning – does not depend on the trajectory and the prior on the trajectories is flat. Equality (4.16) is true under the assumption that all information is carried by the product of the background subtraction and the set of the blob pixel colors. Equality (4.17) is true since $L_t^n = k \Rightarrow X_t^k = 1$, and finally equality (4.18) is true under the assumptions that the occupancy of a location X_t^k provides strictly more information about someone being at location k than the result of the background subtraction, and that given the result of the background subtraction, the color of the blobs does not provide information about the occupancy.

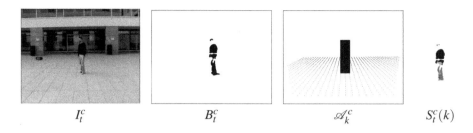

$$I_t^c \qquad\qquad B_t^c \qquad\qquad \mathscr{A}_k^c \qquad\qquad S_t^c(k)$$

Figure 4.2: The color model relies on a stochastic modeling of the color of the pixels $S_t^c(k)$ sampled in the intersection of the binary image B_t^c produced by the background subtraction and the rectangle $\mathscr{A}_k^c$ corresponding to the location k.

4.2.3.5 Color Model

We assume that if someone is present at a certain location k, his presence influences the color of the pixels located at the intersection of the moving blobs and the rectangle $\mathscr{A}_k^c$ corresponding to the location k. We model that dependency as if the pixels were independent and identically distributed and followed a density in the RGB space associated to the individual. This is far simpler than the color models used in either [87] or [61], which split the body area in several sub-parts with dedicated color distributions, but has proved sufficient in practice.

If an individual n was present in the frames preceding the current batch, we have an estimation for any camera c of his color distribution μ_n^c, since we have previously collected the pixels in all frames at the locations of his estimated trajectory. If he is at the hidden location $\mathscr{H}$, we consider that his color distribution μ_n^c is flat.

Let $S_t^c(k)$ denote the pixels taken at the intersection of the binary image produced by the background subtraction from the stream of camera c at time t and the rectangle $\mathscr{A}_k^c$ corresponding to location k in that same field of view (see Fig. 4.2). Note that even if an individual is actually at that location, this intersection can be empty if the background subtraction fails.

Let $\mu_1^c, \ldots, \mu_{N^*}^c$ be the color distributions of the N^* individuals present in the scene at the beginning of the batch of T frames we are processing, for camera c. The distribution may vary with the camera, due to difference in the camera technology or illumination angle.

The ground occupancy term comes from the POM detector, and the color model term is computed as follows.

We have

$$\overbrace{P(L_t^n = k \mid X_t^k = 1, \mathbf{S}_t)}^{\text{Color model}} = \frac{P(L_t^n = k, X_t^k = 1, \mathbf{S}_t)}{P(X_t^k = 1, \mathbf{S}_t)} \tag{4.19}$$

$$= \frac{P(L_t^n = k, X_t^k = 1, \mathbf{S}_t)}{\sum_m P(L_t^m = k, X_t^k = 1, \mathbf{S}_t)} \tag{4.20}$$

$$= \frac{P(L_t^n = k, \mathbf{S}_t)}{\sum_m P(L_t^m = k, \mathbf{S}_t)} \tag{4.21}$$

$$= \frac{P(\mathbf{S}_t \mid L_t^n = k)}{\sum_m P(\mathbf{S}_t \mid L_t^m = k)} \tag{4.22}$$

Equality (4.19) is directly Bayes law, equality (4.20) is true by complementarity of the events $L_t^m = k$, equality (4.21) is true since $L_t^m = k \Rightarrow X_k = 1$, and finally equality (4.22) is true by applying Bayes' law again.

Finally, we have

$$\overbrace{P(L_t^n = k \mid X_t^k = 1, \mathbf{S}_t)}^{\text{Color model}} = \frac{P(\mathbf{S}_t \mid L_t^n = k)}{\sum_m P(\mathbf{S}_t \mid L_t^m = k)} \tag{4.23}$$

where

$$P(\mathbf{S}_t \mid L_t^n = k) = P(S_t^1(k), \dots, S_t^C(k) \mid L_t^n = k) \tag{4.24}$$

$$= \prod_{c=1}^{C} \prod_{r \in S_t^c(k)} \mu_n^c(r). \tag{4.25}$$

4.2.4   Results

In this section, we present different tracking results obtained with our Dynamic Programming-based algorithm on multi-camera pedestrian videos. In our implementation, we first compute the probabilistic occupancy maps of Chapter §3.2 separately at each time step and then use these results as input to our tracker. Since the observed area consists of discrete positions, we improve the result accuracy by linearly interpolating the trajectories on the output images. Figures 4.3, 4.5 and 4.4, illustrate typical tracking results on our multi-camera pedestrian data set.

The performance of the tracker is analyzed in further detail in §4.3.7, page 105, and compared to the Linear Programming-based tracking method of §4.3. Notably, performance figures using the CLEAR metrics are provided there.

4.2.4.1   General Performance

On both indoor *laboratory* sequences, the algorithm performs very well and does not lose a single one of the tracked persons. Results are illustrated by Fig. 4.3.

Figure 4.3: Tracking results on the *laboratory* sequence. Each row displays several views of the same time frame coming from different cameras.

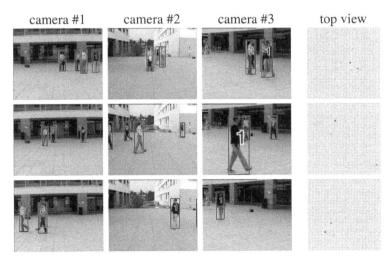

Figure 4.4: Results of the tracking algorithm on the *campus* sequence. Each row displays several views of the same time frame coming from different cameras.

camera #1   camera #2   camera #3   camera #4   top view

Figure 4.5: Tracking results on the *terrace* sequence. Each row displays several views of the same time frame coming from different cameras.

Despite disturbing influence of external elements such as shadows, a sliding door, cars passing by, tables and chairs in the middle of the scene, and the fact that people can enter and exit the tracked area from anywhere on some sequences, the algorithm performs well and follows people accurately on the outdoor *campus* sequence illustrated by Fig. 4.4. In many cases, because the cameras are not located ideally, individuals appear on one stream alone. They are still correctly localized due the POM detector's robustness and the global optimization of the trajectories.

On more challenging sequences from the *terrace* data set, which include at once more than 5 people, illumination changes and similar color clothes, the algorithm starts to make mistakes and mixes some identities or fails to detect people. The main reason is that, as the number of people increases, some people are both occluded on some camera views and out of the range of the other cameras. When this happens for too many consecutive time frames, the dynamic programming is not able to cope with it, and mistakes start to appear.

4.2.4.2 Precision

To further investigate the spatial accuracy of our approach, we compare the estimated locations with the actual locations of the individuals present in the room as follows.

We picked 100 frames at random among a complete sequence and marked by hand a reference point located on the belly of every person present in every camera view. For each frame and each individual, from that reference point and the cali-

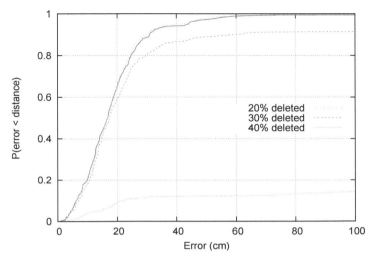

Figure 4.6: Cumulative distributions of the position estimate error on a 3,800-frame sequence. See §4.2.4.2 for details.

bration of the four cameras, we estimated a ground location. Since the 100 frames were taken from a sequence with four individuals entering the room successively, we obtained 354 locations.

We then computed the distance between this ground-truth and the locations estimated by the algorithm. The results are depicted by the bold curve on Fig. 4.6. More than 90% of those estimates are at a distance of less than 31cm and 80% of less than 25cm, which is satisfactory, given that the actual grid resolution is 25cm in these series of experiments.

To test the robustness of our algorithm, for each camera individually, we randomly blanked out a given fraction of the images acquired by that camera. As a result, frames, which are made of all the images acquired at the same time, could contain one or more blank images. This amounts to deliberately feeding the algorithm with erroneous information: Blank images provide incorrect evidence that there was no moving object in that frame, and consequently degrades the accuracy of the occupancy estimate. Hence this constitutes stringent test of the effectiveness of optimizing the trajectories with dynamic programming. The accuracy remains unchanged for an erasing rate as high as 20%. The performance of the algorithm only starts to get noticeably worse when we get rid of one third of the images, as shown in Fig. 4.6. The reason the performance is almost unaltered for erasing rates up to 20% and then suddenly starts to drop is easily understandable: For small erasing rates, POM occupancy maps are slightly less precise and might include some seldom missed detections. The global optimization will still fix the sparse mistaken detections, with a small loss in precision. When the erasing rate increases, so do the missed detection rate and the number of misplaced detections. Above a given threshold, the tracker starts to mistakenly switch identities. After an identity switch, the two switched trajectories will be compared to the wrong ground truth for the rest of the sequence, hence the sudden precision drop.

4.2.5 Discussion

While the algorithm is usually very robust, we discuss here its limitations and potential ways to overcome them.

Entrances and exits As explained in §4.2.2, we deal with people entering and exiting the grid with the help of the virtual location $\mathcal{H}$. This location represents the outside world and is supposed to contain a large number of people, all the people potentially willing to enter our monitored area.

Between consecutive frames, there is a possible transition from the hidden location $\mathcal{H}$ to itself at the next frame, to allow people to stay outside. There is also a possible transition from $\mathcal{H}$ to the grid positions that may act as entrance points, to allow people to enter. For every batch of frames, we first extract trajectories of the people inside the grid. Then, we optimize the trajectory starting from $\mathcal{H}$. If the Dynamic Programming extracts a static trajectory staying in $\mathcal{H}$, it indicates that no new person is entering the grid during the current batch. If however, the trajectory ends up in the grid, the tracker found detections moving from $\mathcal{H}$ to the grid, which is an evidence that someone is entering.

This strategy works very well when the people detector provides accurate results. In most environments, the entrance and exits points are located on the borders of the monitored area and do usually have less good camera coverage than central locations. For this reason, missed detections will more likely occur near an entrance point. Due to the greedy Dynamic Programming optimization, the tracker might miss an entrance if the parts of the trajectory close to $\mathcal{H}$ are not detected. Indeed, if several consecutive miss-detections occur, the static trajectory staying in $\mathcal{H}$ might be less costly than a trajectory that has to pass through several unoccupied locations.

If an entrance is missed that way, the new person will not be tracked, but its detections will nevertheless interfere with the tracking of the other people inside the grid, thus increasing the chances of an identity switch.

The reverse problem can happen for exits: The strategy for dealing with exits is that if an individual's trajectory ends in $\mathcal{H}$ during the current batch, the person is assumed to exit the area, and will not be be tracked in the subsequent batches. Now suppose that a person present in the grid is not detected for a number of consecutive frames. Again due to the greedy nature of the optimizer, the trajectory that quickly joins a hidden location $\mathcal{H}$ and stays there for the duration of the batch might be cheaper than the correct trajectory that stays in the grid during the missed detections. In such a case, we face the same problem as for the missed entrance: The individual that is believed to have exited the grid will still produce future detections, and those might interfere with other trajectories.

These potential problems can be interpreted as a consequence of the greedy strategy of Dynamic Programming framework, and its assymetry between false positives and false negatives treatment. Dynamic Programming carefully avoids false positives - i.e. a trajectory that passes through unoccupied locations - as those are very costly. However, there is no penalty to be paid if some detections remain unexplained by any trajectory. As mentioned at the beginning of this paragraph, this is not a problem when POM detections are accurate, but it makes the tracker less robust in the case they are not. In the next section, we discuss a tracking approach relying on joint optimization of the trajectories, that do not suffer from this issue.

Parameters Our tracking framework relies on several parameters. Most of them are very generic and can be set once. Others might need to be adapted to different environments. The first parameter is the value ρ that determines the average speed of pedestrians in Eq. 4.12. This value was constant for all our pedestrian tracking experiments. However, we had to adapt it when processing the multiple ping-pong ball sequences, whose results are described in §4.4, because the balls are moving significantly faster than pedestrians.

A second parameter is the occupancy probability of the hidden locations $\mathcal{H}$. Although this value does not appear in the formalism of §4.2, a constant occupancy probability must be assigned to the hidden locations, to fully extend the grid model to them. This value must neither be too high, otherwise no person would ever enter or stay in the grid, nor too low to prevent the tracker from creating wrong trajectories every time a false detection appears. In our experience, a value of 0.5 is adequate. When POM detections are noisy, this value may be slightly adapted to prevent the entrance and exit issues discussed above.

The final set of parameters are the size of a batch and the amount of overlap between batches. In all our reported results, we used a batch size of 100 frames and an overlap ratio of 90%. Both values can be substantially reduced when dealing with very good quality detection. Setting those values higher makes the tracking more robust, but increases the computational cost as well as the memory consumption.

Batch processing Processing the values by batches allows for near-real time processing. It is not strictly necessary and one could imagine processing an entire video sequence at once. Note that this way of doing would nevertheless raise some issues about memory consumption and would require some details of the algorithm to be changed, such as the way we handle entrances and exits.

Despite batch processing, the use of global optimization does not allow to process data in real time, strictly speaking, but only in *delayed* real time. Whatever the speed of the computer used for tracking, the algorithm first needs to fill a batch of frames before it can proceed with trajectory extraction. If we process 25 fps videos and use 100-frame batches, this results in a 4 second delay. This means that, at best, the tracking information can be delivered only 4 seconds after the real events happened. This is a limitation that we believe is still suitable for many applications.

In case of very good detections, the batch size can be reduced, but we believe a minimum delay of 1 second - i.e. 25-frame batches - is reasonable and lower values should not be used for best performance.

Independent trajectory optimization   Global optimization of trajectories over a large number of frames is a clear advantage over methods such as Kalman filtering that only link detections between pairs of frames. It provides our method with extra robustness to noisy detections. However, the assumption of independent trajectories is rather strong, and the use of a greedy optimization method exposes our tracker to the danger of trajectories mixing. The use of a confidence score for sorting the individual trajectories optimization is an efficient way to reduce this effect as much as possible. Note that it cannot be suppressed altogether, without considering the joint optimization of all trajectories. In our current framework, the associated complexity would be prohibitive. In the next section, however, we present a different multi-object tracking approach that allows for joint trajectory optimization.

Motion model   Due to the coarse discretization of the grid, we have to accept very fast motions between two successive frames to allow for realistic individual speed over several time frames. This could be overcome with a finer grid, at greater computational cost.

Also, we neither enforce motion consistency along the trajectories nor account for the interactions between people. Greater robustness to potential errors in the occupancy map estimates could therefore be achieved by representing richer state spaces for the people we track and explicitly modeling their interactions. Of course, this would come at the cost of an increased computational burden.

In Chapter 5, we show that the simple isotropic motion model used here can be replaced with a more complex one, learnt from and adapted to a specific environment.

Table 4.3: Notation

K	number of spatial locations;
T	number of time steps;
$\mathbf{I}$	$= (\mathbf{I}_1, \ldots, \mathbf{I}_T)$ captured images;
$\mathcal{N}(k)$	$\subset \{1, \ldots, K\}$ neighborhood of location k;
$e_{i,j}^t$	directed edge from location i at time t to location j at time $t + 1$;
$f_{i,j}^t$	estimated number of objects moving from location i at time t to location j at time $t + 1$;
m_i^t	estimated number of objects at location i at time t;
M_i^t	random variable standing for the true number of objects at location i at time t;
$\mathfrak{F}$	set of occupancy maps physically possible;
$\mathfrak{H}$	set of flows physically possible, i.e. satisfying the constraints of Eqs. 4.26, 4.27, 4.28, and 4.35.

4.3 Multiple People Tracking with Flow Linear Programming

In this section, we introduce a second approach to tackle the multi-people tracking problem, using as input the detection maps of POM. We design a generic and mathematically sound multiple object tracking framework that relies on Linear Programming. This allows us to perform a joint optimization of several trajectories, and thus avoid some of the pitfalls faced by the Sequential Dynamic Programming approach from the previous section. Our new method depends on very few parameters and the algorithm handles unknown and potentially changing number of objects while naturally filtering out false positives and bridging gaps due to false negatives.

4.3.1 Overview

We first formulate multi-target tracking as an Integer Programming (IP) problem. Although such a problem is usually NP-complete, in our case a relaxation of it as a Linear Program yields the optimal solution, and hence the problem is efficiently solvable. In a second step, we illustrate how the k-shortest paths algorithm [117] can be used to solve our specific framework much more efficiently than generic Linear Programming solvers. We discuss these steps in more detail below and will use notation summarized in Table 4.3.

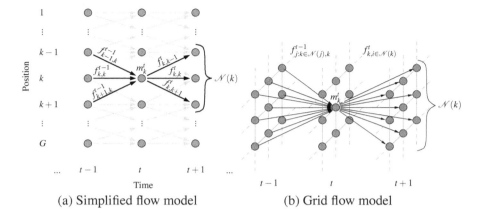

(a) Simplified flow model   (b) Grid flow model

Figure 4.7: (a) Simplified flow model, which does not use a virtual position. Positions are arranged on one dimension and neighborhood is reduced to 3 positions. (b) Flow model used for tracking objects moving on a 2-D grid, such as in pedestrian tracking. For the sake of readability, only the flows to and from location k at time t are printed.

4.3.2 Formalization

The physical area of interest is discretized into K locations, and the time interval into T instants. For any location k, let $\mathcal{N}(k) \subset \{1, \ldots, K\}$ denote the neighborhood of k, that is, the locations an object located at k at time t can reach at time $t+1$.

To model occupancy over time, let us consider a labeled directed graph with KT vertices, which represents every location at every instant. Its edges correspond to admissible object motions, which means that there is one edge $e_{i,j}^t$ from (t,i) to $(t+1, j)$ if, and only if, $j \in \mathcal{N}(i)$. To allow objects to remain static, there is always an edge from a location at time t to itself at time $t+1$.

Each vertex is labeled with a discrete variable m_i^t standing for the number of objects located at i at time t. Each edge is labeled with a discrete variable $f_{i,j}^t$ standing for the number of objects moving from location i at time t to location j at time $t+1$, as shown in Fig. 4.7(a). For instance, the fact that an object remains at location i between times t and $t+1$ is represented by $f_{i,i}^t = 1$.

Given these definitions, for all t, the sum of flows arriving at any location j is equal to m_j^t, which also is the sum of outgoing flows from location j at time t. We must therefore have

$$\forall t, j, \quad \underbrace{\sum_{i : j \in \mathcal{N}(i)} f_{i,j}^{t-1}}_{\text{Arriving at } j \text{ at } t} = m_j^t = \underbrace{\sum_{k \in \mathcal{N}(j)} f_{j,k}^t}_{\text{Leaving from } j \text{ at } t} . \tag{4.26}$$

Furthermore, since a location cannot be occupied by more than one object at a time, we can set an upper-bound of 1 to the sum of all outgoing flows from a given location and impose

$$\forall k, t, \quad \sum_{j \in \mathcal{N}(k)} f_{k,j}^t \leq 1. \tag{4.27}$$

A similar constraint applies to the incoming flows, but we do not need to explicitly state it, since it is implicitly enforced by Eq. 4.26. Finally, the flows have to be positive and we have

$$\forall k, j, t, f_{k,j}^t \geq 0. \tag{4.28}$$

Note that constraints (4.27) and (4.28) implicitly enforce that the flows $f_{k,j}^t$ are smaller or equal to 1, which is consistent with our model.

Let M_i^t denote a random variable standing for the true presence of an object at location i at time t. The object detector used to process the sequence provides, for every location i and every instant t, an estimate of the marginal posterior probability of the presence of an object

$$\rho_i^t = \hat{P}(M_i^t = 1 \,|\, \mathbf{I}_t), \tag{4.29}$$

where $\mathbf{I}_t$ is the signal available at time t. For the multi-camera pedestrian-tracking application, $\mathbf{I}_t$ denotes the series of pictures taken by all the cameras at time t.

Let $\mathbf{m}$ be an occupancy map, that is a set of occupancy variables m_i^t, one for each location and for each instant. We say that $\mathbf{m}$ is *feasible* if there exists a set of flows $f_{k,j}^t$ that satisfies Eqs. 4.26, 4.27, and 4.28, and we define $\mathfrak{F}$ the set of feasible maps. Our goal then becomes solving

$$\mathbf{m}^* = \arg\max_{\mathbf{m} \in \mathfrak{F}} \hat{P}(\mathbf{M} = \mathbf{m} \,|\, \mathbf{I}) \ . \tag{4.30}$$

Assuming conditional independence of the M_i^t, given the $\mathbf{I}_t$, the optimization problem of Eq. 4.30 can be re-written as

$$\mathbf{m}^* = \arg\max_{\mathbf{m} \in \mathfrak{F}} \log \prod_{t,i} \hat{P}(M_i^t = m_i^t \,|\, \mathbf{I}_t) \tag{4.31}$$

$$= \arg\max_{\mathbf{m} \in \mathfrak{F}} \sum_{t,i} \log \hat{P}(M_i^t = m_i^t \,|\, \mathbf{I}_t)$$

$$= \arg\max_{\mathbf{m} \in \mathfrak{F}} \sum_{t,i} (1 - m_i^t) \log \hat{P}(M_i^t = 0 \,|\, \mathbf{I}_t)$$

$$\qquad\qquad + m_i^t \log \hat{P}(M_i^t = 1 \,|\, \mathbf{I}_t) \tag{4.32}$$

$$= \arg\max_{\mathbf{m} \in \mathfrak{F}} \sum_{t,i} m_i^t \log \frac{\hat{P}(M_i^t = 1 \,|\, \mathbf{I}_t)}{\hat{P}(M_i^t = 0 \,|\, \mathbf{I}_t)} \tag{4.33}$$

$$= \arg\max_{\mathbf{m} \in \mathfrak{F}} \sum_{t,i} \left(\log \frac{\rho_i^t}{1 - \rho_i^t} \right) m_i^t, \tag{4.34}$$

where Eq. 4.31 is true under the assumption of conditional independence of the M_i^t given I_t, Eq. 4.32 is true because m_i^t is 0 or 1 according to Eq. 4.27, and Eq. 4.33 is obtained by ignoring a term which does not depend on **m**. Hence, the objective function of Eq. 4.34 is a linear expression of the m_i^t. Note that since we use the POM detector in our experiments, the assumption of conditional independence of the M_i^t for (4.31) is legitimate, since the ρ_i^t are specifically estimated by POM so that the corresponding product law mimics the true joint posterior.

In general, the number of tracked objects may vary with time, meaning that objects may appear inside the tracking area and others may leave. Thus, the total mass of the system changes and we must allow flows to enter and exit the area.

We do this by introducing two additional nodes v_{source} and v_{sink} into our graph, which are linked to all the nodes representing positions through which objects can respectively enter or exit the area, such as doors or borders of the camera field of view. In addition, a flow goes from v_{source} to all the nodes of the first frame, and reciprocally a flow goes from all the nodes of the last frame to v_{sink}. We call v_{source} and v_{sink} *virtual locations*, because, as opposed to the other nodes of the graph, they do not represent any physical location.

Finally, we introduce an additional constraint that ensures that all flows departing from v_{source} eventually end up in v_{sink}

$$\underbrace{\sum_{j\in\mathcal{N}(v_{source})} f_{v_{source},j}}_{\text{Leaving } v_{source}} = \underbrace{\sum_{k:v_{sink}\in\mathcal{N}(k)} f_{k,v_{sink}}}_{\text{Arriving at } v_{sink}} . \tag{4.35}$$

4.3.3 Optimization

We optimize with respect to the flows $f_{i,j}^t$ rather than the occupancies m_i^t, because there is no natural way to express the flow continuity constraints in terms of the latter. We therefore solve the following Integer Programming problem, that incorporates the constraints of Eqs. 4.26, 4.27, 4.28, and 4.35:

$$
\begin{aligned}
\text{Maximize} \quad & \sum_{t,i} \log\left(\frac{\rho_i^t}{1-\rho_i^t}\right) \sum_{j\in\mathcal{N}(i)} f_{i,j}^t \\
\text{subject to} \quad & \forall t,i,j,\ f_{i,j}^t \geq 0 \\
& \forall t,i,\ \sum_{j\in\mathcal{N}(i)} f_{i,j}^t \leq 1 \\
& \forall t,j,\ \sum_{i:j\in\mathcal{N}(i)} f_{i,j}^{t-1} = \sum_{k\in\mathcal{N}(j)} f_{j,k}^t \\
& \sum_{j\in\mathcal{N}(v_{source})} f_{v_{source},j} = \sum_{k:v_{sink}\in\mathcal{N}(k)} f_{k,v_{sink}} .
\end{aligned}
\tag{4.36}
$$

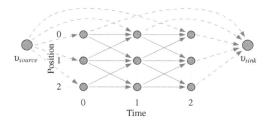

Figure 4.8: A complete flow system for a simple graph consisting only of 3 positions and 3 time frames. Here, we assume that position 0 is connected to the virtual positions and therefore a possible entrance and exit point. Flows to and from the virtual positions are shown as dashed lines.

This is equivalent to maximizing the objective function of Eq. 4.34 because $\forall t, j, m_j^t = \sum_{k \in \mathcal{N}(j)} f_{j,k}^t$. In other words, we simply replace all the m_j^t in the original formulation by the sum of the outgoing flows from j at time t, so that the unknowns are now the flows.

We rewrite the system of Eq. 4.36 in *canonical form* with inequality constraints instead of equalities:

$$
\begin{aligned}
\text{Maximize} \quad & \sum_{t,i} \log\left(\frac{\rho_i^t}{1 - \rho_i^t}\right) \sum_{j \in \mathcal{N}(i)} f_{i,j}^t \\
\text{subject to} \quad & \forall t, i, j, \ f_{i,j}^t \geq 0 \\
& \forall t, i, \quad \sum_{j \in \mathcal{N}(i)} f_{i,j}^t \leq 1 \\
& \forall t, i, \quad \sum_{j \in \mathcal{N}(i)} f_{i,j}^t - \sum_{k:i \in \mathcal{N}(k)} f_{k,i}^{t-1} \leq 0 \\
& \quad \sum_{j \in \mathcal{N}(v_{source})} f_{v_{source},j} - \sum_{k:v_{sink} \in \mathcal{N}(k)} f_{k,v_{sink}} \leq 0 \ .
\end{aligned}
\tag{4.37}
$$

This new formulation is strictly equivalent to the one of Eq. 4.36 and no additional constraint is needed. The inequalities are indeed sufficient to ensure that no flow can ever appear or disappear within the graph. An example of a complete graph is illustrated in Fig. 4.8.

Under this formulation, our Integer Program can be solved by any generic LP solver. However, due to the very large size of our problem, this solution would hardly be practical, as IP solving is NP-complete. The usual workaround is to relax the integer assumption and solve a continuous Linear Program instead, which has polynomial-time average-case complexity. The drawback of this method is that the Linear Program is unlikely to converge to the optimal solution of the original IP.

In our case, however, the relaxed Linear Program always converges towards an integer solution, due to the very specific form of our constraints. The complete proof can be found in [11]. As a consequence, we can use generic LP solver to optimize our multi-target tracking framework. Nevertheless, although this approach is tractable for moderately sized problems, it is still too slow for most practical applications. Therefore, in the next section, we propose another method for performing the optimization, which takes into account the specificity of our problem to tremendously reduce the complexity.

4.3.4   K-Shortest Paths Formulation

The relaxation of the original integer problem yields a large scale LP problem, which can be solved by several state-of-the-art LP solvers, such as CPLEX [55], GLPK [79] and MATLAB [81], that, in general, rely on variants of the Simplex algorithm [27] or interior point based methods [62]. However, these algorithms do not make use of the specificity of our problem and have very high worst case time complexities. In the following, we show that this complexity can be reduced considerably by reformulating the problem as a *k shortest node-disjoint paths* problem on a directed acyclic graph (DAG).

Given a pair of nodes, namely the source v_{source} and the sink v_{sink}, in a graph G, the k-shortest paths problem is to find the k paths $\{p_1, \ldots, p_k\}$ between these nodes, such that the total cost of the paths is minimum. The problem is well-studied in the network optimization literature and the results have been widely applied in the field of network connection routing and restoration. There exists many variants of the algorithm, each targeted at a specific problem instance [1].

In our specific case, we are interested in the particular instance where the graph is directed and paths are both node-disjoint - i.e. two separate paths cannot share the same node - and node-simple - i.e. a path visits every node in the graph at most once. We use the graph structure with a single source and a single sink illustrated by Fig. 4.8. Any path between v_{source} and v_{sink} in this graph represents the flow of a single object in the original problem along the edges of the path. The node-disjointness constraint means that no location can be shared between two paths, hence two objects. This is thus equivalent to the constraint of Eq. 4.27. Moreover, since we only look for paths between the source and sink nodes, we ensure that no flow can ever be created nor suppressed anywhere else in the graph than at the virtual locations, which enforces the constraints of Eqs. 4.26 and 4.35. Finally, the node-simple characteristic of the paths simply stems from the fact that our graph is a DAG, hence acyclic.

A directed edge $e_{i,j}^t$ from location i at time t to location j at time $t+1$ is assigned

---

[1]for a complete list of references, see the online bibliography at http://liinwww.ira.uka.de/bibliography/Theory/k-path.html

the cost value

$$c(e_{i,j}^t) = -\log\left(\frac{\rho_i^t}{1-\rho_i^t}\right). \tag{4.38}$$

The cost value of the edges emanating from the source node is set to zero to allow objects to appear at any entrance position and at any time instant at no cost. We formulate our problem as a minimization problem by negating the objective function of Eq. 4.36.

Let $\mathfrak{H}$ denote the set of feasible solutions of the original LP formulation of Eq. 4.36, satisfying the constraints given in Eq. 4.26, 4.27, 4.28, and 4.35. Then, the optimal solution $\mathbf{f}^*$ of the k-shortest path problem can be written as

$$\mathbf{f}^* = \arg\min_{\mathbf{f} \in \mathfrak{H}} \sum_{t,i} c(e_{i,j}^t) \sum_{j \in \mathcal{N}(i)} f_{i,j}^t \quad, \tag{4.39}$$

where $c(e_{i,j}^t)$ represents the cost of the edge $e_{i,j}^t$ as defined in Eq. 4.38. Note that any node-disjoint k paths between v_{source} and v_{sink} with arbitrary k is in the feasible set of solutions $\mathfrak{H}$. In addition, any solution in $\mathfrak{H}$ can be expressed as a set of k node-disjoint paths.

Let p_i^* be the shortest path computed at the ith iteration of the algorithm and $P_l = \{p_1^*, \ldots, p_l^*\}$ be the set of all l shortest paths computed up to iteration l. We start by finding the single shortest path in the graph p_1^* and compute its total cost

$$\text{cost}(p_l^*) = \sum_{e_{i,j}^t \in p_l^*} c(e_{i,j}^t). \tag{4.40}$$

We then compute iteratively the l-shortest paths for $l = 2, 3, 4, \ldots$, and for each l, we calculate the total cost of the shortest paths

$$\text{cost}(P_l) = \sum_{i=1}^{l} \text{cost}(p_i^*). \tag{4.41}$$

At each new iteration $l+1$, the total cost $\text{cost}(P_{l+1})$ is compared to the cost at the previous iteration $\text{cost}(P_l)$. The optimal number of paths k^* is obtained when the cost of iteration k^*+1 is higher than the one of iteration k^*. The procedure is summarized by the pseudo-code of Algorithm 1, page 150.

To compute such k-shortest paths, we use the *disjoint paths* algorithm [117], which is an efficient iterative method based on signed paths. For the sake of completeness, we give a brief description of this algorithm in Appendix A.

The equivalence of the LP and the k-shortest paths formulations follows from the exact procedure we use to select an optimal k such that the objective function is minimized. Since path costs are monotonically increasing

$$\text{cost}(p_{i+1}^*) \geq \text{cost}(p_i^*) \qquad \forall i, \tag{4.42}$$

the optimal number of objects k^* is only discovered at iteration $k^* + 1$. Therefore, the cost function is convex with respect to the variable l and the global minimum satisfies the condition

$$cost(P_{k^*-1}) \geq cost(P_{k^*}) \leq cost(P_{k^*+1}), \qquad (4.43)$$

which is set as a stopping criterion in the algorithm, as shown in Algorithm 1. Finally, among the set of all consecutive values that may satisfy the above condition, we select the smallest one to avoid erroneous splitting of paths.

The total time complexity of the algorithm is $O(k(m + n \cdot \log n))$, where k is the number of objects appearing in a given time interval, m is the number of edges and n is the number of nodes in the final transformed graph (see Appendix A for details). This is much faster than general LP solvers, and a gain in speed of up to a factor 1,000 can be expected, as illustrated by the run time comparison in §4.4.3.

4.3.5   Further Complexity Reduction

As discussed above, the number of variables of our optimization problem is high. When needed, two simple techniques can be used to significantly reduce it.

Pruning the Graph   Most of the probabilities of presence estimated by the detector are virtually equal to zero. We can use this sparsity to reduce the number of nodes to consider in the optimization, thus reducing the computational cost. In other words, given loose upper bounds on the speed of the objects to track and on the maximum number of false negatives the detector can produce successively, we can build a criterion to remove nodes of the graph which are very unlikely to ever be occupied.

Formally, for every position k and every frame t, we check the maximum detection probability within a given spatio-temporal neighborhood

$$\max_{\substack{\|j-k\|<\tau_1 \\ t-\tau_2<u<t+\tau_2}} \rho_j^u . \qquad (4.44)$$

If it is found to be below a threshold, the location is considered as unused because no object could reach it with any reasonable level of probability. All flows to and from it are then removed from the model. Applying this method allows us to reduce the number of variables and constraints up to an order of magnitude.

Batch Processing   Instead of directly optimizing a whole video sequence, one can separate it into several batches of frames and optimize over them individually. To enforce temporal consistency across batches, we add the last frame of the previously optimized batch to the current one. We then force the flows out of every location of this frame to sum up to the location's value in the previous batch

$$\forall k \in \{1, \ldots, K\}, \quad \sum_{j \in \mathcal{N}(k)} f_{k,j}^{-1} = \mu_k, \tag{4.45}$$

where μ_k is the score at location k of the last frame of the previous batch and $f_{k,j}^{-1}$ is a flow from location k of the last frame of the previous batch to location j in the first frame of the current batch. This is implemented as an additional constraint in our framework.

4.3.6 Algorithm Output

Estimating the $f_{i,j}^t$ indirectly provides the m_i^t values and the feasible occupancy map $\mathbf{m}^*$ of maximum posterior probability. This data can be used as a cleaned up version of the original occupancy map, in which most false positives and negatives have been filtered out.

However, the $f_{i,j}^t$ themselves provide, in addition to the instantaneous occupancy, estimates of the actual motions of objects. From these estimated flows of objects, one can follow the motion back in time by moving along the edges whose $f_{i,j}^t$ are not 0, and build the corresponding long trajectories.

4.3.7 Results

In this section, we present results of our tracking algorithm in two very different contexts. First, we apply it on the standard multi-camera setup to track pedestrians. The frequent occlusions between people produce noisy detections, which our algorithm nevertheless links very reliably. As a result, our approach was shown to compare favorably against other state-of-the-art algorithms in the PETS 2009 evaluation [34]. Second, to highlight the fact that this new algorithm does not use an appearance model, we track sets of similar-looking bouncing balls seen from above. Throughout this section, we compare the Linear Programming-based tracker to the Dynamic Programming framework described in §4.2.

4.3.7.1 Test Data

We evaluate the two tracking methods on some of our multi-camera pedestrian data sets for which we have labelled a ground truth. Those include various environments: a 6-person *laboratory* sequence, a crowded outdoor sequence of the *terrace* data set as well as 4 sequences from the very difficult *passageway* data set, which corresponds to a realistic video-surveillance scenario, with all associated shortcomings. Additionally, we also perform our own detailed evaluation on one of the sequences

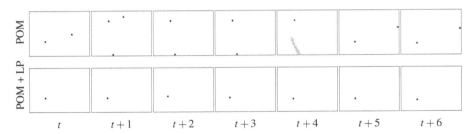

Figure 4.9: Original probabilistic occupancy maps for 7 consecutive frames of a *passageway* sequence (upper row) compared to the output of the Linear Programming algorithm (lower row). The darker the color, the higher the probability of presence. Note that the POM maps are extremely noisy, as evidenced by the fact that the number of probability peaks and their locations vary wildly. By contrast, only one peak remains in the LP output, and it moves slowly, which is consistent with the motion of a person over 1/4th of a second.

from the PETS 2009[2] data set. Furthermore, we make a second series of tests on a very different environment: tracking sets of similar-looking bouncing balls filmed from above by a single camera. This is an environment were the Dynamic Programming's color model does not help. All these test scenarios are depicted by Figs. 2.9 and 2.10, and described in details in §2.7 on page 24 and followings.

Note that the characteristics of the *passageway* sequence - bad lighting, uneven camera coverage - greatly affect the quality of the probabilistic occupancy maps we use as input. As illustrated by Fig. 4.9, the detection maps can be very noisy, with some people wrongly located or simply ignored for significant numbers of consecutive frames. On these noisy sequences, if we were to detect people by simply thresholding the maps in individual frames, the true positive rate would drop to 70% to 80%, thus making the linking task challenging.

In the rest of this section, we refer to the Linear Programming framework as 'LP', to the LP solved using the k-shortest paths algorithm of §4.3.4 as 'KSP', and to the sequential Dynamic Programming as 'DP'.

4.3.7.2   Probabilistic Occupancy Map

We used the Probabilistic Occupancy Map algorithm to create the detection data needed as input by our trackers. POM specifically estimates the the marginal posterior probability ρ_k^t of presence of a target at a location, such that the resulting product law closely approximates the joint posterior distribution, which justifies the assumption of conditional independence in Eq. 4.31.

To process the monocular sequence of bouncing balls, we modified slightly the original POM silhouette model to represent the balls as squares and work directly in

---

[2]Eleventh IEEE International Workshop on Performance Evaluation of Tracking and Surveillance, Miami, June 2009, http://pets2009.net

the top view, without having to project from oblique images into it. This adaptation is explained in details in Chapter 3.2.5.

4.3.7.3 Pedestrian Tracking Results

For pedestrians tracking, we define the graph of Fig. 4.7(a) as follows: Every interior location of the ground plane at time t is linked to its 9 direct neighbors at time $t + 1$, as illustrated by Fig. 4.7(b), which means that a pedestrian can only move from one location to its immediate neighbors between consecutive frames. Border locations through which access to the area is possible are connected to the virtual locations v_{source} and v_{sink}. This arrangement is consistent with our chosen grid quantization at 25 fps, and even suits the 7 fps PETS 2009 sequence, since the pedestrians are not moving fast. Should we deal with even lower frame rate, or objects moving faster, we could easily modify this model to extend the neighborhood size, as explained below in §4.3.7.6. Detection results for all evaluated sequences are shown on Fig. 4.10, and tracking results on Fig. 4.11. Both DP and KSP trackers are represented on those figures.

Detection and tracking precision metrics (MODP and MOTP) roughly gauge the quality of the bounding box alignment, in the cases of correct detection. Since both DP and KSP link POM detections together, their precision score rarely exceeds the one of POM itself, although it may happen that the interpolation performed by the trackers corrects some misalignment of POM, such as in the *laboratory* sequence of Fig. 4.10(a). However, in both detection and tracking precision, KSP almost always achieves significantly higher scores than DP.

The detection accuracy metrics (MODA) evaluates the relative number of false positives and missed detections. Note that DP is often lower than POM, because it tends to ignore trajectories for which some detections were missed, and thus produces more missed detections. By contrast, KSP generally outperforms POM and almost always DP. By accurately linking detections together, while discarding isolated alarms, KSP efficiently filters the detections results, effectively decreasing both the false positives and missed detections counts.

Finally, the tracking accuracy measure (MOTA) is very similar to the detection one (MODA), except for the fact that it also takes identity switches into account. Not surprisingly, KSP again scores higher than DP. Examples of tracking results are illustrated on Figs. 4.13 to 4.16.

Please recall that KSP uses only POM occupancy maps, whereas DP also looks at the original images and maintains a color model per tracked individual. In other words, KSP produces better results, even though it requires less information. This is valuable, because, in some situations such as the ball tracking presented below, appearance models cannot be depended upon.

4.3.7.4   Precision

To quantify the precision of the generated tracks, we proceed as described in §4.2.4.2. A precise ground truth was generated for 100 frames extracted at random from a *laboratory* sequence with 4 people. The distance on the ground plane between the ground truth and the tracker detections are then computed and their cumulative distribution is plotted by the bold curve in Fig. 4.12.

The result is very similar to the one obtained by the Dynamic Programming method and displayed in Fig. 4.6. This is not surprising: when the detection true positive rate is high, the detection precision is mainly determined by POM. The trackers are merely linking detections together.

When input frames are randomly blanked, however, we notice that the Linear Programming results are less affected than the ones from the Dynamic Programming. This is consistent with the tests from §4.4, in which LP is shown to be more resistant than DP to miss-detections.

4.3.7.5   Monocular Pedestrian Results

To further emphasize the strength of our approach, we generated the detection maps using only one of the 7 available views of the PETS data set. Although POM still works on monocular sequences, the ground plane localization is intrinsically less precise. Without several views from different angles, there is an inherent depth ambiguity when estimating a pedestrian's position, especially when the background subtraction blobs are noisy or incomplete. Also, in the monocular case, occlusions often result in missed detections.

Under these challenging conditions, the Linear Programming algorithm shows its superiority over the sequential Dynamic Programming, even more clearly than in the multi-camera case. This is illustrated by Figs. 4.10 and 4.11. In this context, DP's greedy strategy often prefers leaving people outside the grid rather than trying to explain the very noisy detections. By contrast, KSP's joint optimization pays off and interpolates trajectories nicely. These monocular tracking results are depicted by Fig. 4.17.

4.3.7.6   Ball Tracking Results

Given the difference in grid scale, the balls move much faster than pedestrians, easily travelling more than one grid location between consecutive frames. In this context, keeping the same neighborhood model as for pedestrian tracking would lead both DP and KSP trackers to miss most balls. Therefore, to deal with this environment, we had to extend the location neighborhood to include the next closest 49 locations, which limits the maximum distance travelled between consecutive frames to 3 grid locations.

Detection and tracking results for the two ball sequences are also illustrated on Figures 4.10 and 4.11. Detecting ping-pong balls does not represent a particularly difficult task, and the POM results are generally excellent, with very few false positives and false negatives. Because all balls have exactly the same appearance, DP's color model is useless and the comparison between the two algorithms is fairer. As evidenced by Figs. 4.10 and 4.11, KSP outperforms DP on all of the 4 metrics. Here again, DP's greedy strategy is a disadvantage. Because it might be less costly to leave some detections unexplained, DP tends to leave out too many of them. Example results are shown on Fig. 4.18.

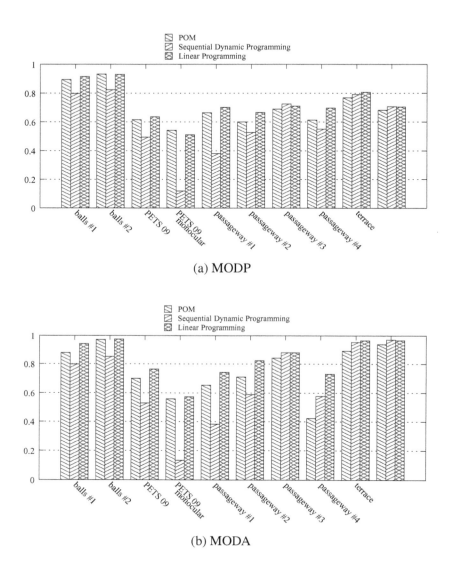

(a) MODP

(b) MODA

Figure 4.10: Detection precision (MODP) and accuracy (MODA) measures applied to the results of the original detection (POM), as well as the sequential Dynamic Programming (DP) and the proposed Linear Programming based (KSP) trackers on various sequences.

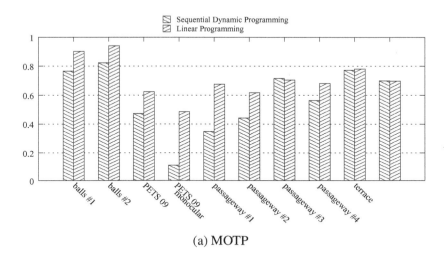

(a) MOTP

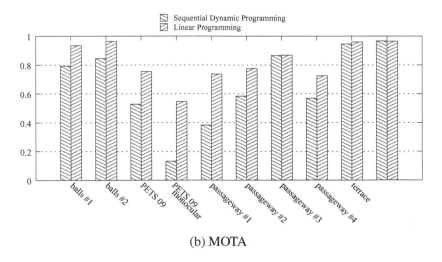

(b) MOTA

Figure 4.11: Tracking precision (MOTP) and accuracy (MOTA) measures applied to the results of the sequential Dynamic Programming (DP) and the proposed Linear Programming based (KSP) trackers on various sequences.

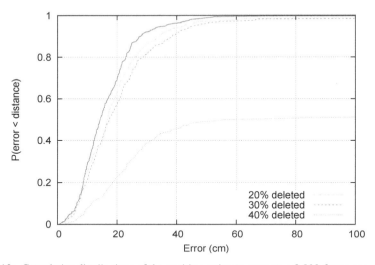

Figure 4.12: Cumulative distributions of the position estimate error on a 3,800-frame sequence. See §4.2.4.2, page 92 for details.

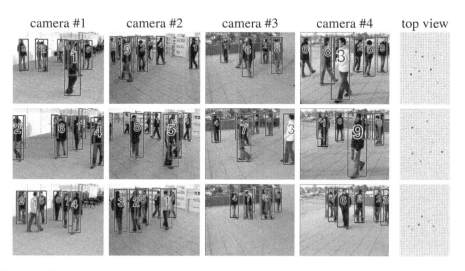

Figure 4.13: Multi-camera pedestrian tracking results on two video sequences of the *terrace* data set. Each of the first four columns shows a different camera view. The fifth column displays the top view.

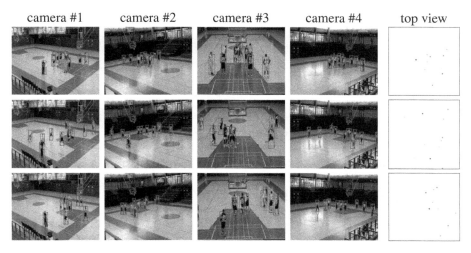

Figure 4.14: Multi-camera pedestrian tracking results on the *basket* video sequence. Each of the first four columns shows a different camera view. The fifth column displays the top view.

Figure 4.15: Multi-camera pedestrian tracking results on the *passageway* data set. Each of the first four columns shows a different camera view. The fifth column displays the top view.

camera #1   camera #3   camera #4   camera #5   top view

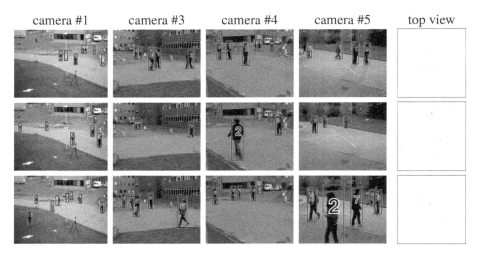

Figure 4.16: Multi-camera pedestrian tracking results on the PETS 2009 data set. Each of the first four columns shows a different camera view. The fifth column displays the top view.

Figure 4.17: Some monocular pedestrian tracking results, from the PETS 2009 sequence. The first row displays 4 screen shots of the camera view used for tracking and the second row shows the corresponding top view detections.

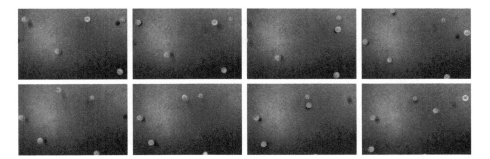

Figure 4.18: Multiple ball tracking results. Successive screenshots are separated by 3 time frames.

4.4   Discussion

In this section, we further evaluate and compare our Dynamic Programming and Linear Programming-based tracking methods from §4.2 and §4.3 respectively. For readability, we denote as *DP* the Dynamic approach, *LP* the Linear Programming one and *KSP* the Linear Programming solved with the k-shortest paths algorithm. Note that *LP* and *KSP* always produce exactly the same results. The difference is that *KSP* obtains them much faster.

4.4.1   PETS 2009

The results of our two tracking approaches on the PETS 2009 S2/L1 multi-camera tracking sequence have been submitted for evaluation to the Winter-PETS 2009 workshop. The results of this comparative evaluation are presented in [34] and illustrated by Fig. 4.19. They show that, for the tracking task, our Linear Programming based approach outperforms the other submitted methods. Nevertheless, our Dynamic Programming-based approach is also shown to perform well.

4.4.2   Detailed Evaluation

Here, we run a series of tests to quantify the robustness of the two tracking algorithms developed in this chapter with respect to various elements.

4.4.2.1   False Detections

First, to test how the trackers react to false detections, we ran the following experiment: We selected a 1500-frame excerpt from a *laboratory* sequence, in which 4 people are successively entering the room. We specifically chose a passage in which the POM detection accuracy is high - MODA score of more than 0.92 - which means that the number of false positives and negatives is very low. We then artificially added false detections into the POM score. The wrong detections were added uniformly over the whole grid, and at every location and time frame independently, thus representing white noise. The resulting occupancy maps are depicted by Fig. 4.20. The correct detections were not affected by this process. Both tracking algorithms were applied to the corrupted POM occupancy maps, for various amounts of false positives.

The result of the analysis is displayed on the left graph of Fig. 4.21(a), which plots the MODA score for increasing false detection rates. Both algorithms have a stable performance up to a certain noise value, beyond which the accuracy quickly drops. DP is more robust than LP and is not affected by up to 22% of false detections, whereas LP accuracy starts decreasing around 5% already.

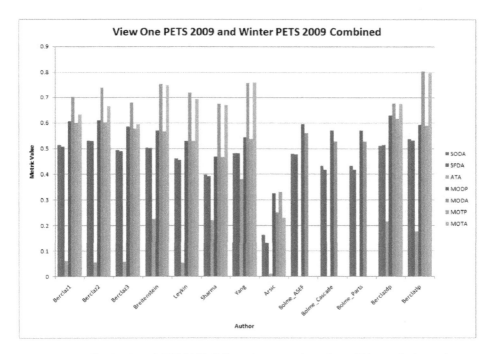

Figure 4.19: Official Winter-PETS 2009 [34] results comparison chart. This graph shows the performance of the different tracking methods submitted to the workshop on the S2/L1 sequence. The results are evaluated with the CLEAR and VACE [63] metrics, briefly described in Chapter 2.6. In the chart, POM is referred to as 'Berclaz1' to 'Berclaz3'. For those three labels, slightly different parameters were used. The Dynamic Programming algorithm is referred to as 'Berclazdp' and the Linear Programming approach as 'Berclazlp'. Figure courtesy of James Ferryman and Ali Shahrokni from the Computational Vision Group, University of Reading.

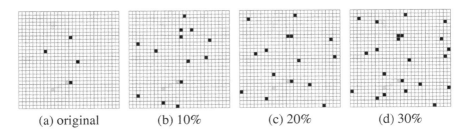

| (a) original | (b) 10% | (c) 20% | (d) 30% |

Figure 4.20: Illustration of the amount of false detections added to the original POM occupancy maps to generate Fig. 4.21.

The graph of Fig. 4.21(b) gives more insight on the behavior of the trackers when fed with false detections. For both methods, the true positives are not affected by the noise. The false positives, however increase suddenly. The reason is quite intuitive: beyond a density of false positives, the tracking algorithms are able to link them into (wrong) trajectories. The higher the density, the larger the number of false trajectories. Below this threshold, false detections are simply discarded. Here, LP's lack of a motion model is a disadvantage over DP. Conversely, DP's tendency to leave out incomplete trajectories makes it more robust to this kind of noise.

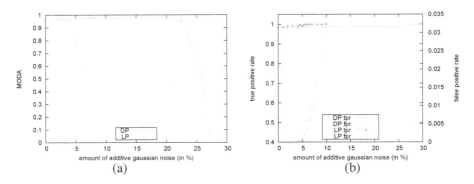

Figure 4.21: Influence of false detections on tracking algorithms. A 1,500-frame sequence from the *laboratory* data set with up to 4 people was processed by POM, yielding close to perfect detections (MODA higher than 0.92). False detections were then added randomly to the POM results, following a uniform independent distribution. On the left graph (a), the detection accuracy of both the DP and LP methods applied to the noisy POM data is plotted for various amounts of noise. The right graph (b) plots the true and false positive rates for the same input.

4.4.2.2 Missed Detections

In a second test, we investigate the effect of missed detections on the general performance of the trackers. The same clip of the *laboratory* sequence as for the previous test was used. This time, however, we post-processed POM occupancy maps by randomly canceling detections. Again, this is done independently at every frame and every detection.

Figure 4.22(a) displays the MODA detection accuracy score for the corrupted POM maps, as well as for the DP and LP tracker results. Not surprisingly, the probability maps accuracy is linearly decreasing with the amount of cancelled detections. As for the previous test about false positives, the two trackers react very differently. LP's performance is almost unaffected for as high a rate as 70% dropped detections. By contrast, DP's score already starts decreasing for 5% of missing detections and completely collapses at about 15%.

The graph of Fig. 4.22(b) shows that the treatment applied to POM detection maps only affects the true positive rate, and does not concern the false positive one. Both detectors react the same way to missed detections: beyond a threshold, the remaining detections are no longer linked together and remain unexplained. LP shows nevertheless a much higher robustness to missed detections than DP does. This is consistent with our observation on real data: on Figs. 4.10 and 4.11, one can generally notice that the lower POM occupancy maps quality, the higher the gap between DP and LP performance. Furthermore, it confirms the discussion of DP limitations with regard to entrances and exits in §4.2.5.

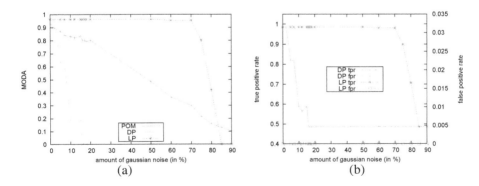

Figure 4.22: Influence of missed detections on the tracking algorithms. A 1,500-frame sequence from the *laboratory* data set with up to 4 people was processed by POM, yielding close to perfect detections (MODA higher than 0.92). Detections were then suppressed randomly. The right graph (a) plots the detection accuracy of the noisy POM data as well as DP and LP applied to it, for various amounts of noise. The right graph (b) plots the true and false positive rates for the same noise values.

4.4.2.3   Image Quality

Next, we apply the two trackers on the occupancy maps obtained from the images corrupted with noise, described in Chapter 3.2.6. The first set of noisy images was generated by adding Gaussian flip noise to background subtraction images and the second by altering the foreground blobs with Gaussian noise. The effects are illustrated by Figs. 3.18 and 3.20 on page 55.

Results for both tracking methods are shown by the graphs of Fig. 4.23 for the flip noise and Fig. 4.24 for the noise on foreground blobs. On both tests, the two tracking methods perform almost identically. In the two cases, the drop of performance is mainly triggered by the quick fall of detection true positives that can be observed in Figs. 3.19 and 3.22 on page 55.

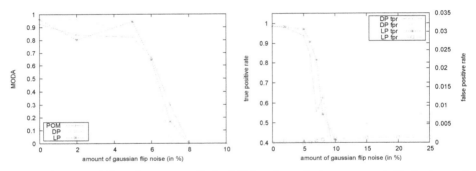

Figure 4.23: DP and LP trackers were applied to POM results on the images corrupted by background noise from Figs. 3.18 and 3.20. Not surprisingly both trackers are equally affected.

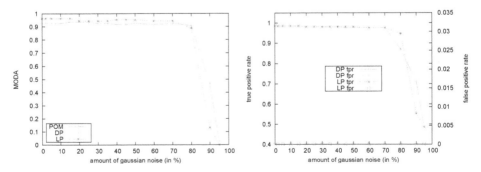

Figure 4.24: DP and LP trackers were applied to POM results on the images whose foreground blobs were corrupted by noise (see Figs. 3.21 and 3.23). The corresponding detection results for both trackers are plotted along with those from POM.

4.4.2.4 Number of Cameras

The final robustness test concerns the number of cameras used for the occupancy map generation. Two 4-camera sequences (*laboratory* and *terrace*) as well as a 6-camera one (PETS 09) were processed by POM, with decreasing number of cameras. The detection evaluation is presented in Chapter 3.2.6.

Here we apply the two trackers introduced in this chapter to the detection maps obtained with various numbers of cameras. The results evaluated with the MODA and MOTA metrics are shown on Figs. 4.25 and 4.26 respectively. Note that the two metrics yield almost similar results, indicating that identity switches are not a concern here. The result shows that the Linear Programming approach is more robust than DP when processing sequences filmed by a small number of cameras. For the *laboratory* and *terrace* sequences, both methods yield almost the same performance with 4 cameras, but the gap widens rapidly when the number of cameras decreases.

Note that the order at which cameras were removed might slightly influence the result, as some camera views sometimes cover the scene better, or are more precisely calibrated than others.

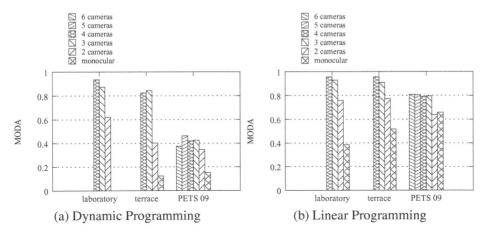

(a) Dynamic Programming   (b) Linear Programming

Figure 4.25: Influence of the number of cameras on DP and LP's performance. Three test sequences have been processed by the POM detector using a decreasing number of camera views (see Fig. 3.25). DP and LP tracking algorithm have been in turn applied to this detection data.

4.4.3 Run time

Finally, we evaluate the speed of our tracking algorithms. Solving the Linear Program with standard LP libraries is slow, as shown in the graph of Fig. 4.27 under the label *LP*, for which we used a standard LP package [79]. Using the complexity

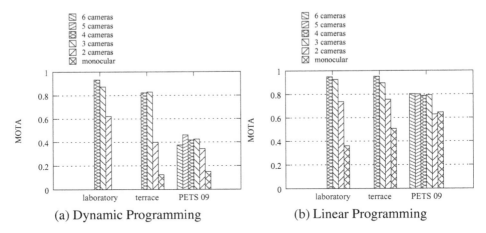

(a) Dynamic Programming   (b) Linear Programming

Figure 4.26: Influence of the number of cameras on DP and LP's performance. Three test sequences have been processed by the POM detector using a decreasing number of camera views (see Fig. 3.25). DP and LP tracking algorithm have been in turn applied to this detection data.

reduction method of §4.3.5 helps reduce the computation time by a factor of 10, as shown by the curve labeled *LP w/ compl. red.*. Here, we pruned the graph using a radius of $\tau_1 = \tau_2 = 3$ (see Eq. 4.44).

By contrast, the solver based on the k-shortest paths algorithm is much faster. As illustrated on Fig. 4.27 by the curve *KSP*, there is a considerable speed gain of a factor 100 to 1,000, compared to the generic LP solver [79]. And the gain is still very significant even when complexity reduction methods are applied to the standard LP solver.

Compared to the DP algorithm, KSP is about 10 times faster, as shown on Fig. 4.27. Note that DP suffers from the fact that it has to load videos, in order to maintain its appearance models. The batches overlap is an additional overhead that penalizes DP. Interestingly, when dealing with 25 fps videos, KSP can in average process a batch of frames in less than half the time it takes to record it. This means that, for a frame rate of 25 fps or less, our tracker can easily run in real time.

All the above experiments have been performed on a recent Linux PC, equipped with a 2.5 GHz Intel processor and 8 GB of memory. Tracking was applied to a part of the *laboratory* sequence, in which 5 to 7 people are present. For the k-shortest path, no particular optimization was performed, nor did we use any of the complexity reduction methods of §4.3.5. The results of DP and KSP on Fig. 4.27 are the average of 20 runs, plotted with 95% confidence interval. This is barely noticeable because the values are very peaked around the average.

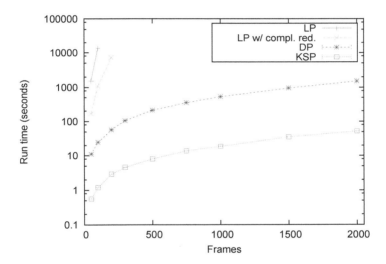

Figure 4.27: Runtime comparison between LP solved with a generic package (LP), LP with a pruned graph solved by a generic package (LP w/ comp. red.), DP and LP solved with the k-shortest paths algorithm (KSP). For 'DP' and 'KSP', the respective algorithms have been run 20 times on every tested batch, and the average is plotted in the above graph, along with 95% confidence intervals (barely noticeable due to very peaked values around the average). Note that the y axis represents run time and is plotted in log scale.

Chapter 5

Behavior analysis

In recent years, there has been a rapid rise of the number of CCTV cameras installed in public places. In the city of London alone, where the video-surveillance phenomenon is particularly strong, the number of working cameras has been estimated to more than 500,000 already by 2006 [84, 93]. And this amount is certainly following a constant growth.

Such a large number of cameras is generating a tremendous amount of data, whose processing remains an open problem. Therefore, most of the cameras are currently being used as passive prevention devices: Whether active or not, visible cameras are expected to discourage common misbehaving such as theft or violence, at least within the limits of their field of view. Furthermore, those cameras can reveal very useful *a posteriori*, for example by providing a recorded sequence for a criminal investigation. However, the real time monitoring of the video data produced by the CCTV cameras is such a complex task that it is currently only feasible by a human operator. This solution is far from optimal, because people can monitor efficiently only a small number of video feeds simultaneously. Moreover the human attention span is limited over time and it is difficult and exhausting for a person to focus for an extended period of time on several screens.

For those reasons, automated analysis of surveillance data is receiving growing attention recently. It is clear that the current state of research is not mature enough to produce a complete video understanding solution, but a technology able to pre-filter the video by drawing the attention of an operator to the potentially eventful environments would already prove extremely useful. This may permit to relieve a human operator from the burden of low-level monitoring, and let him concentrate on the more critical task of decision making, which, whatever the state of the technology, we may not be ready to entrust to a computer.

The complete pedestrian detection and tracking framework from multiple views that we have developed in Chapters 3 and 4 lends itself very well to the behavior analysis task. The precise ground plane localization that it can provide represents the perfect type of input data for a system whose task is to automatically learn the most common motion patterns followed in a given environment, and potentially recognize the trajectories departing too much from the standard model.

In this chapter we therefore propose an approach to automatically learning a number of so-called *behavioral maps*, using as only input the detection maps generated by POM. Those behavioral maps represent a model for the main types of movement observed in the monitored area. We show that this model can be learnt in an unsupervised manner, and is powerful enough to automatically detect abnormal trajectories. Furthermore, we demonstrate that the proposed behavioral maps integrate very well with the Dynamic Programming-base tracking approach of Chapter 4.2, and can be used to effectively replace the simple isotropic motion model by a more sophisticated one, yielding better tracking results.

5.1   State-of-the-Art

With the advent of video surveillance and real-time people tracking algorithms, we have recently seen an increasing amount of research focused on acquiring spatio-temporal patterns by passive observation of video sequences [60, 113, 9, 80, 53], as well as sociology-oriented studies about general pedestrian dynamics [51, 50, 106, 108].

Various techniques have been proposed for clustering pedestrian trajectories and build a behavior model of an observed environment. The corresponding approaches usually rely on a people tracker to provide with the basic trajectory observation, and then group them into different possible motion patterns. For example, [101] performs on-line clustering of trajectories and represents them with a hierarchical tree structure. [90] first reduces the trajectories dimensionality using discrete Fourier transform and clusters them with a Self Organizing Map algorithm. Similarly, [3] relies on PCA for dimensionality reduction, followed by trajectories clustering using fuzzy mean-shift. In [21], trajectories are represented as a sequence of directions and modeled as a Von Mises distribution. The authors employ a K-medoids clustering technique to build a mixture of Von Mises distributions. Finally, [98] groups similar trajectories using a hierarchical clustering algorithm. While efficient, all these approaches expect correct trajectories to be readily available, which may not be straightforward to obtain. By contrast, the method presented in this chapter just needs simple time-independent detections as input.

Our approach shares similarities with [60], since we try to learn trajectory distributions from data as they do. However, while they model the trajectories in the camera view, and handle the temporal consistency using an artificial neural network with a short memory, we propose a more straightforward modeling under a classical Markovian assumption with an additional behavioral hidden state. The metric homogeneity of the top-view allows for simpler priors, and the resulting algorithm can be integrated seamlessly in a standard HMM-based tracking system, such as our Dynamic Programming-based tracker.

In a relatively close spirit, [113] uses an adaptive background subtraction algorithm to collect patterns of motion in the camera view. With the help of vector quantization, they build a codebook of representations out of this data, which they use to detect unusual events. [139] also relies on initial background subtraction, and build paths by linking foreground blobs. At a later stage, the paths are clustered and interpolated using splines. [80] proceeds in a similar fashion to gather statistics from an online surveillance system. Using this data, they infer higher level semantics, such as the locations of entrance points, stopping areas, etc.

More related to our approach is the work of [9], which applies an E-M algorithm to cluster trajectories recorded with laser-range finders. From this data, they derive an HMM to predict future position of the people. The use of laser-range scanners and their trajectory cluster model makes this approach more adapted to an indoor environment where people have a relatively low freedom of movement, whereas our proposed behavioral maps are more generic and learned from standard video sequences shot with off-the-shelf cameras. Similarly, [2] characterizes crowd behavior by observing the crowd optical flow and uses unsupervised feature extraction to encode normal crowd behavior. PCA is applied to extract motion models, which are combined through an HMM.

A quite different approach to behavior modeling has been chosen by [5, 4]. Instead of learning a scene-wide behavior model from image data, they focus on the individual level and hand-design a pedestrian behavior model based on Discrete Choice Models, whose parameters are estimated from real tracking results. The model is then introduced as prior knowledge inside a people tracking framework. As opposed to our method, this approach focuses on the generic individual pedestrian behavior, and does not adapt to the specificities of a particular environment.

Finally, our approach to handling human behaviors can be seen as a simplified version of Artificial Intelligence techniques, such as Plan Recognition [19] where the strategies followed by the agents are encoded by the behavioral maps. This simplification is what lets us learn our models from real data without having to hand-design them, which is a major step-forward with respect to traditional Artificial Intelligence problems.

5.2 Atypical Motion Detection using Behavioral Maps

In this section, we introduce models that can both describe how people move on a location of interest's ground plane, such as a cafeteria, a corridor, or a train station, and be learned from image data. To validate these models, we use the POM people detector to learn them and our Dynamic Programming-based tracker to demonstrate that they can help disambiguate difficult situations. We also show that, far from forcing everyone to follow a scripted behavior, the resulting models can be used to detect abnormal behaviors, which are defined as those that do not conform to our expectations. This is a crucial step in many surveillance applications whose main task is to raise an alarm when people are having dangerous or prohibited behavior.

Figure 5.1: The approach presented in this section uses the output of the POM detector to learn several *behavioral maps* encoding the most likely types of movements observed in an environment.

We represent specific behaviors by a set of *behavioral maps* that encode, for each ground plane location, the probability of moving in a particular direction. We then associate to people being tracked a probability of acting according to an individual map and to switch from one to the other based on their location. The maps and model parameters are learned by Expectation-Maximization in a completely unsupervised fashion. At run-time, they are used for robust and near real-time recovery of trajectories in ambiguous situations. Also, the same maps are used for efficient detection of abnormal behavior by computing the probability of retrieved trajectories under the estimated model. We show that the models we propose are both sophisticated enough to capture higher-level behaviors that basic Markovian models cannot, and simple enough to be learned automatically from training data.

In the remainder of this section, we present the core algorithm of our approach, first by describing the formal underlying motion model, and second by explaining both the E-M training procedure and the method through which the adequate training data was collected.

5.2.1   Motion Model

As briefly described above, our motion model relies on the notion of behavioral map, a finite hidden state associated to every individual present in the scene. The rational behind that modeling is that an individual trajectory can be described with a deterministic large scale trajectory both in space and time (i.e. "he is going from door

A to door B", "he is walking towards the coffee machine") combined with additional noise. The noise itself, while limited in scale, is highly structured: motion can be very deterministic in a part of a building where people do not collide, and become more random in crowded area. Hence this randomness is both strongly anisotropic – people in a certain map go in a certain direction – and strongly non-stationary – depending on their location in the area of interest the fluctuations differ. With an adequate class of models for individual maps, combining several of them allows for encoding such a structure.

Hence, re-using the formalism of Chapter 2, we associate to each individual a random process (L_t, M_t) indexed by the time t and taking its values in $\{1, \ldots, K\} \times \{1, \ldots, M\}$ where $K \simeq 1000$ is the number of locations in the finite discretization of the area of interest and M is the total number of behavioral maps we consider, typically less than 5. We completely define this process by first making a standard Markovian assumption, and then choosing models for both $P(L_0, M_0)$ and

$$P(L_{t+1}, M_{t+1} \mid L_t, M_t) \ . \tag{5.1}$$

Note that the very idea of maps strongly changes the practical effect of the Markovian assumption. For instance, by combining two maps that encode motions in opposite directions and a very small probability of switching from one map to the other, the resulting motion model is a mixture of two flows of individuals, each strongly deterministic. By making the probabilities of transition depend on the location, we can encode behaviors such as people changing their destination and doing a U-turn only at certain locations. Such a property can be very useful to avoid confusion of the trajectories of two individuals walking in opposite directions.

To define precisely (5.1), we first make an assumption of conditional independence between the map and the location at time $t + 1$ given the same at time t

$$P(L_{t+1}, M_{t+1} \mid L_t, M_t) = P(L_{t+1} \mid L_t, M_t) P(M_{t+1} \mid L_t, M_t) \ . \tag{5.2}$$

Due to the 25 cm spatial resolution of our discretization, we have to consider a rather coarse time discretization to be able to model motion accurately. If we were using directly the frame-rate of 25 time steps per second, the location at time $t + 1$ would be almost a Dirac mass on the location at the previous time step. Hence, we use a time discretization of 0.5 s, which has the drawback of increasing the size of the neighborhood to consider for $P(L_{t+1} \mid L_t, M_t)$. In practice an individual can move up to 4 or 5 spatial locations away in one time step, which leads to a neighborhood of more than 50 locations.

The issue to face when choosing these probability models is the lack of training data. It would be impossible for instance to model these distributions exhaustively as histograms, since the total number of bins for $K \simeq 1,000$ and $M = 2$, if we consider transitions only to the 50 spatial neighbor locations and all possible maps, would be $\simeq 1,000 * 2 * 50 * 10 = 10^6$, hence requiring that order of number of observations. To cope with that difficulty, we interpolate these mappings with a Gaussian kernel from a limited number Q of control points, hence making a strong assumption of spatial regularity.

Finally, our motion model is totally parameterized by fixing the locations $l_1, \ldots, l_Q \in \{1, \ldots, K\}^Q$ of control points in the area of interest (where Q is a few tens), and for every point l_q and every map m by defining a distribution $\mu_{q,m}$ over the maps and a distribution $f_{q,m}$ over the locations.

From these distributions, for every map m and every location l, we interpolate the distributions at l from the distributions at the control points with a Gaussian kernel κ:

$$P(L_{t+1} = l', M_{t+1} = m' \,|\, L_t = l, M_t = m)$$
$$= P(L_{t+1} = l' \,|\, L_t = l, M_t = m) P(M_{t+1} = m' \,|\, L_t = l, M_t = m) \qquad (5.3)$$
$$= \left\{ \frac{\sum_q \kappa(l, l_q) f_{q,m}(l - l')}{\sum_r \kappa(l, l_r)} \right\} \left\{ \frac{\sum_q \kappa(l, l_q) \mu_{q,m}(m')}{\sum_r \kappa(l, l_r)} \right\} . \qquad (5.4)$$

Remains the precise definition of the motion distribution itself $f_{q,m}(\delta)$, for which we still have to face the scarcity of training data compared to the size of the neighborhood. We decompose the motion δ into a direction and a distance and make an assumption of independence between those two components:

$$f_{q,m}(\delta) = P(L_{t+1} - L_t = \delta \,|\, L_t = l_q, M_t = m) \qquad (5.5)$$
$$= g_{q,m}(\|\delta\|) h_{q,m}(\theta(\delta)) , \qquad (5.6)$$

where $\|.\|$ denotes the standard Euclidean norm, g is a Gaussian density, θ is the angle quantized in eight values and h is a look-up table, so that $h(\theta(.))$ is an eight-bin histogram.

Finally, the complete parameterization of our model requires, for every control point and every map, M transition probabilities, the two parameters of g and the eight parameters of h, for a total of $Q * M * (M + 2 + 8)$ parameters.

5.2.2 Training

We present in this part the training procedure we use to estimate the parameters of the model described in the previous section. We denote by α the parameter vector of our model (of dimension $Q * M * (M + 2 + 8)$) and index all probabilities with it.

Provided with images from the video cameras, the ultimate goal would be to optimize the probability of the said sequence of images under a joint model of the image and the hidden trajectories, which we can factorize into the product of an appearance model (i.e. a posterior on the images, given the locations of individuals) with the motion model we are modeling here. However, such an optimization is intractable. Instead, we use an *ad-hoc* procedure to extract trajectory fragments from the probabilistic occupancy maps of the POM detector, and to optimize the motion model parameters to maximize the probability of those fragments.

5.2.2.1   Generating the Fragments.

To produce the list of trajectory fragments we will use for the training of the motion model, we first apply the POM algorithm to every frame independently. We then threshold the resulting probabilities with a fixed threshold to produce finally at every time step t a small number N_t of locations $(l_1^t, \ldots, l_{N_t}^t) \in \{1, \ldots, K\}^{N_t}$ likely to be truly occupied.

To build the fragments of trajectories we process pairs of consecutive frames and pick the location pairing $\Xi \subset \{1, \ldots, N_t\} \times \{1, \ldots, N_{t+1}\}$ minimizing the total distance between paired locations $\sum_{\xi \in \Xi} ||l_{\xi_1}^t - l_{\xi_2}^{t+1}||$. If $N_t > N_{t+1}$, some points occupied at time t cannot be paired with a point at time $t + 1$, which corresponds to the end of a trajectory fragment. Reciprocally, if $N_t < N_{t+1}$, some points occupied at $t + 1$ are not connected to any currently considered fragment, and a new fragment is started.

We end up with a family of U fragments of trajectories

$$\mathbf{f}_u \in \{1, \ldots, K\}^{S_u}, \quad u = 1, \ldots, U \ . \tag{5.7}$$

5.2.2.2   E-M Learning.

The overall strategy is an E-M procedure which maximizes alternatively the posterior distribution on maps of every point of every fragment $\mathbf{f}_u$, and the parameters of our motion distribution.

Specifically, let $\mathbf{f}_u^k$ denote the k-th point of fragment u in the list of fragments we actually observed. Let $\mathbf{F}_u^k$ and M_u^k denote respectively the location and the hidden map of the individual of fragment u at step k under our model.

Then, during the E step, we re-compute the posterior distribution of those variables under our model. For every first point of a fragment, we set it to the prior on maps. For every other point we have:

$$v_u^k(m)$$
$$= P_\alpha(M_u^k = m \mid \mathbf{F}_u^1 = \mathbf{f}_u^1, \ldots, \mathbf{F}_u^k = \mathbf{f}_u^k) \tag{5.8}$$
$$= \sum_{m'} P_\alpha(M_u^k = m \mid \mathbf{F}_u^{k-1} = \mathbf{f}_u^{k-1}, \mathbf{F}_u^k = \mathbf{f}_u^k, M_u^{k-1} = m') \, v_u^{k-1}(m') \tag{5.9}$$
$$\propto \sum_{m'} \underbrace{P_\alpha(\mathbf{F}_u^k = \mathbf{f}_u^k \mid \mathbf{F}_u^{k-1} = \mathbf{f}_u^{k-1}, M_u^{k-1} = m')}_{\text{motion model of map } m'}$$
$$\cdot \underbrace{P(M_u^k = m \mid \mathbf{F}_u^{k-1} = \mathbf{f}_u^{k-1}, M_u^{k-1} = m')}_{\text{transition probability from map } m' \text{ to } m, \text{ at location } \mathbf{f}_u^{k-1}} \, v_u^{k-1}(m') \tag{5.10}$$
$$= \sum_{m'} \left\{ \frac{\sum_q \kappa(\mathbf{f}_u^{k-1}, l_q) f_{q,m'}(\mathbf{f}_u^{k-1} - \mathbf{f}_u^k)}{\sum_r \kappa(\mathbf{f}_u^{k-1}, l_r)} \right\} \left\{ \frac{\sum_q \kappa(\mathbf{f}_u^{k-1}, l_q) \, \mu_{q,m'}(m)}{\sum_r \kappa(\mathbf{f}_u^{k-1}, l_r)} \right\} v_u^{k-1}(m') \ .$$
$$\tag{5.11}$$

From this estimate, during the M step, we recompute the parameters of $\mu_{q,m}$ and $f_{q,m}$ for every control point l_q and every map m in a closed-form manner, since there are only histograms and Gaussian densities. Every sample $\mathbf{f}_u^k$ is weighted with the product of the posterior on the maps and the distance kernel weight $v_u^k(m) \, \kappa(\mathbf{f}_u^k, l_q)$.

5.3 Results

In this section, we describe the behavioral models we learned first from synthetic data, and then from multi-camera pedestrian video sequences. We demonstrate how they can be used both to improve the reconstruction of typical trajectories and to detect atypical ones.

5.3.1 Synthetic Data

The first step taken to validate the correct functioning of our algorithm was to test it against synthetic data. We generated synthetic probabilistic occupancy maps of people moving along predefined paths, an example of which is shown in Fig. 5.2. New people were created at the beginning of paths according to a Poisson distribution. Their speed followed a Gaussian distribution and their direction of movement was randomized along the paths. When two or more paths were connected, we defined transition probabilities between them, and people were switching paths accordingly.

The results on the synthetic data have been fully satisfying, as the retrieved behavioral maps correctly reflected the different paths we created. As an example, Fig. 5.3 illustrates the 4 motion maps obtained when applying our algorithm to the scenario of Fig. 5.2, while Fig. 5.4 depicts the probabilities of transition between

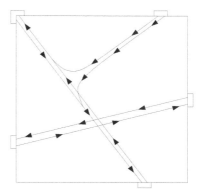

Figure 5.2: A scenario used to generate synthetic occupancy maps for testing. People move along the edges between entrance and exit points.

maps. A careful observation of the motion maps reveals that they are sufficient to encode all possible movements allowed by the initial scenario. Furthermore, when performing cross-validation, we verify that 4 represents indeed the ideal number of maps for this scenario, as illustrated by the graph of Fig. 5.5.

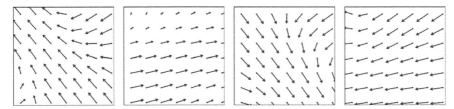

Figure 5.3: The four motion maps retrieved when applying our algorithm to synthetic occupancy data modeled according to the scenario of Fig. 5.2. We can see that those maps are sufficient to encapsulate all the possible movements from the initial scenario.

5.3.2 Training Sequences

To test our algorithm, we used the multi-camera *behavior* data set described in Chapter 2.7, which comprises two different sequences. The first video sequence, which lasts about 15 minutes, is used for training purposes. It features four people walking in front of the cameras, following the predefined patterns of Fig. 5.6 that involve going from one entrance point to another.

In a second 8-minute-long test sequence, the same 4 people follow the patterns of Fig. 5.6 for about 50 percent of the time and take randomly chosen trajectories for the rest. These random movements can include standing still for a while, going in

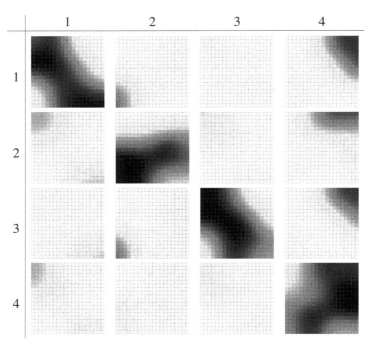

Figure 5.4: Transition probabilities between the movement maps of Fig. 5.3. Dark color indicates a high probability.

and out of the area through non standard entrance points, taking one of the predefined trajectory backwards, etc. Screen shots of the test sequence with anomaly detection results are displayed on Fig. 5.12.

5.3.3   Behavior Model

As described in § 5.2.2, we first apply the POM people detector on the video streams, which yields ground plane detections that are used by our E-M framework to construct the behavior model.

The ground plane of the training sequence is discretized into a regular grid of 30×45 locations. Probability distribution maps are built using one control point every 3 locations. The behavioral model of the 15 minute long training sequence is generated using 30 E-M iterations, which takes less than 10 minutes on a 3 GHz PC using no particular optimization.

We use cross-validation to choose the number of maps that gives the most significant model. We apply our learning algorithm several times on 80% of the training sequence with each time a different number of maps, as shown on Fig. 5.7. The rest

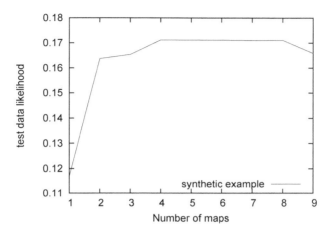

Figure 5.5: Cross-validation on the synthetic example of Fig. 5.2. We see that the ideal number of behavioral maps for this scenario is 4, which corresponds to the results of Fig. 5.3.

of the sequence is used to compute the likelihood of the trajectories under our model. In the end, we choose the smallest number of maps, which accurately captures the patterns of motion. On our testing sequence, it turns out that two maps are already sufficient. Figure 5.8 displays the behavioral maps that are learned in the one-map (left) and two-map (right) cases. By comparing them to Fig. 5.6, one can see that the two-map case is able to model all trajectories of the scenario.

Figure 5.9 shows the probabilities of staying in the same behavioral map over the next half second. These probabilities are relatively high, but not uniform over the whole ground plan, which indicates that people are more likely to switch between maps at some locations.

5.3.4 Tracking Results

Here, we discuss the benefits of using behavioral maps learned with our algorithm to improve the performance of a people tracker. To this purpose, we replace the uniform isotropic motion model of the Dynamic Programming-based people tracker of Chapter 4.2 with our learned behavioral maps.

The behavioral maps had to be adapted to fit into the Dynamic Programming framework. Specifically, from every behavioral map, we generated a motion map that stores, for each position of the ground plane, the probability of moving into one of the adjacent positions at the next time frame.

The main difference with the original Dynamic Programming tracker is that a hidden state in the HMM framework is now characterized by both a map and a position.

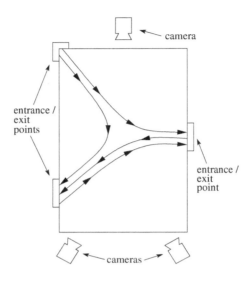

Figure 5.6: Top view of the scenario used for algorithm training. People are going from one entrance point to an exit point using one of the available trajectories.

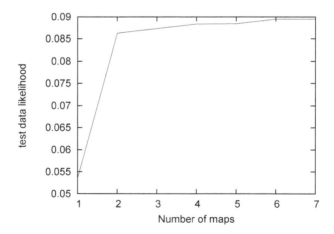

Figure 5.7: Cross-validation: to find the ideal number of maps to model a given scenario, we run our learning algorithm with different number of maps on 80% of the training sequence. We then use the other 20% to compute the likelihood of the data given our model. In our training sequence, that is shown here, 2 maps are enough to model the situation correctly.

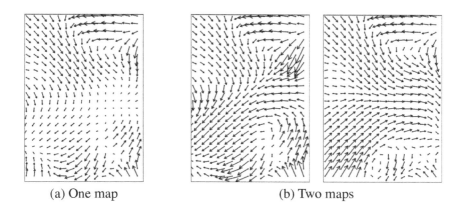

(a) One map   (b) Two maps

Figure 5.8: Motion maps in the top view resulting from the learning procedure, with one map (a) or two maps (b). The difficulty of modeling a mixture of trajectories under a strict Markovian assumption without an hidden state appears clearly at the center-right and lower-left of (a): Since the map has to account for motions in two directions, the resulting average motion is null, while in the two-map case on (b) two flows appear clearly.

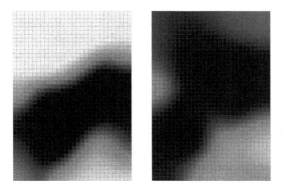

Figure 5.9: Probability to remain in the map 0 (left) and in the map 1 (right) in the two-map case. Dark color indicates a high probability.

Table 5.1: The false negative value corresponds to the number of trajectories out of a total of 75, that were either not found or were not consistent with the ground truth. The false positive value stands for the average number of false detections per time frame.

	$R = .5\text{m}$		$R = 1\text{m}$		$R = 2\text{m}$	
	FN	FP	FN	FP	FN	FP
Original DP	17	0.18	14	0.15	13	0.15
Behavior, one map	15	0.22	13	0.20	12	0.19
Behavior, two maps	10	0.21	10	0.18	10	0.17

Also the transition between HMM states is now given by both a transition probability between maps and between locations. The rest of the tracking framework, however, has been untouched.

To quantify the benefits of the behavioral maps, we started by running the original tracker on our training sequence. We then ran the modified version on the same sequence, using in turn a one-map behavior model and a two-map one.

A ground truth used to evaluate the results was derived by manually marking the position and identity of each person present on the ground plane once every 10 frames. Scores for both algorithms were then computed by comparing their results to the ground truth. For this purpose, we define a trajectory as being the path taken by a person from the time it enters the area until it exits it. For every trajectory of the ground truth, we search if there is a matching set of detections from the algorithm results. A true positive is declared when, for every position of a ground truth trajectory, a detection is found within a given distance R, and all detections correspond to the same identity. If there is a change in identity, it obviously means that there has been a confusion between the identities of two people, which cannot be considered as a true positive. The false positive value is the average number of false detections per time frame. Results from Table 5.1 show both false positive and negative values for the original and the modified algorithm using a one-map and a two-map behavior model. Results are shown for 3 different values of the distance R.

It appears from Table 5.1 that for about the same number of false positives, using 1, respectively 2, behavioral maps helps reducing significantly the number of false negatives. Moreover, one can notice that the paths are found with greater precision, when using two behavioral maps, since the number of false negatives is no longer influenced by the distance R.

The behavioral maps were only integrated with the Dynamic Programming-based tracker, for which an obvious fit exists. In the scope of this work, we did not attempt to adapt our Linear Programming-based tracker to make it compatible with a motion model derived from behavioral maps. This is however a potential extension and an

Table 5.2: Error rate for atypical trajectory detection. The total number of retrieved trajectories is 47, among which 16 are abnormal. With either one or two maps, the number of false positives (i.e. trajectories flagged as abnormal while they are not) drops to 1 for a number of false-negatives (i.e. non flagged abnormal trajectories) greater than 2. However, for very conservative thresholds (less than 2 false-negatives) the two-map model the advantage of using two maps appears clearly.

FN	FP	
	One map	Two maps
0	29	9
1	7	4
2	1	1

interesting direction for future work.

5.3.5 Anomaly Detection Results

Detecting unlikely motions is another possible usage of the behavioral maps computed by our algorithm. We show the efficiency of this approach by applying it for classifying trajectories from the test sequence into "normal" or "unexpected" category.

We start by creating a ground truth for the test sequence. We manually label each trajectory depending on whether it follows the scenario of Fig. 5.6 or not.

For every trajectory, a likelihood score is computed using the behavioral maps. For this we proceed using an HMM framework, in which our hidden state is the behavioral map the person is following. The transition between states is given by the transition probabilities between maps and the observation probability is the probability of a move, given the map the person is following. Having defined all this, the likelihood of a trajectory is simply computed using the classical forward-backward algorithm. The score is then compared to a threshold to classify the trajectory as "normal" or "unexpected".

We classified the 47 trajectories automatically retrieved from the test sequence using a one-map and a two-map behavior models. The results are displayed on Table. 5.2 and show the improvement when using several maps: the behavior model with only one map produces 7 (respectively 29) false positives if missing only one (respectively zero) abnormal trajectories, when the two-map models reduces this figure to 4 (respectively 9).

Instead of computing a score for a complete trajectory, one can also generate a score for a small part of it only, using the very same technique. This way of doing is more appropriate for monitoring trajectories in real time, for instance embedded in a tracking algorithm. This leads to a finer analysis of a trajectory, where only the unexpected parts of it are marked as such.

This procedure can be used directly to "tag" individuals on short time interval in the test video sequence. Figure 5.11 shows a selected set of atypical behavior, according to our two-map model. The unlikely parts of the trajectories are drawn using dotted-style lines. This should be compared to the two right maps of Fig. 5.8. On the other hand, Fig. 5.10 shows some trajectories that follow the predefined scenario. Finally, Fig. 5.12 illustrates the same anomaly detection results, projected on camera views.

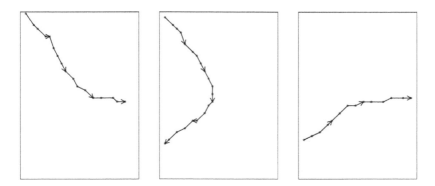

Figure 5.10: Three example of retrieved "normal" trajectories, according to the scenario illustrated on Fig. 5.6.

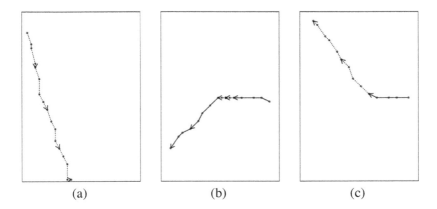

Figure 5.11: Three examples of retrieved atypical trajectories, according to the scenario illustrated on Fig. 5.6. Unlikely parts are displayed with dotted-style lines. a) The person is taking an unusual path; b) The person is stopping (middle of the trajectory); c) The person is taking a predefined path backward.

Figure 5.12: Anomaly detection in camera views. Each row consists of views from three different cameras at the same time frame. A red triangle above a person indicates that it does not move according to the learned model.

Chapter 6

Conclusion

In this book, we have presented a vision system capable of detecting multiple people, tracking them and learning their most common movement patterns in a specific environment. The approach was designed to work with multiple static off-the-shelf cameras located at about 2 m above the ground.

We have shown that our mathematically sound detection framework deals naturally with occlusions, heavy noise and monocular situations, yielding metrically accurate detections at independent time frames, by just using binary images from background subtraction. Furthermore, we have sketched a classification-based detection scheme to bypass a limitation of our first detection method and distinguish pedestrians from other moving objects.

In a second step, we demonstrated that global optimization is well suited to link detections produced by a people detector at individual time frames. A first attempt involved using Dynamic Programming on occupancy maps along with color and motion models to extract trajectories that were assumed independent. We then reformulated the multi-object tracking problem as a constrained flow optimization, whose structure is very simple and which can be solved using standard Linear Programming. We alleviated the usual burden of joint optimization by designing a technique based on the k-shortest paths algorithm, that was specifically adapted to the sparse structure of our problem and allowed us to solve it extremely fast.

In a last step, we created a new model for representing typical pedestrian motions in a particular environment. This model consists of a set of behavioral maps, each of which encodes a different type of observed behaviour. Relying on E-M, we showed that our model can be learnt from detection data in an unsupervised way. We demonstrated different usages of this data: It represents a sophisticated motion model designed for a specific environment and can be integrated into a people tracker to make it more robust. Besides, it can be used to analyze trajectories and detect abnormal ones.

6.1 Applications

Some parts of the system developed in this work have already been used in various projects. For instance, the POM people detector has been integrated into the large "Dynamic Visual Network" of the European project "DYVINE"[1]. Inside this consortium, POM has been deployed for monitoring an area with multiple cameras. The detector was connected to a larger framework gathering information coming from various sensors and presenting an intuitive situation summary to be used by a human operator. Our system was generating alarms whenever people entered some pre-defined restricted areas, and sending them to the central framework, along with the coordinates of the detected people.

Our complete detection and tracking system was also integrated within the Swiss National Research Foundation Project "Aerial Crowd". It was used to track multiple people inside a typical urban environment. The positions of people were then transmitted to an Augmented Reality system that used them to customize the scene with virtual actors.

The POM detector is currently integrated into the *Idiap Showroom*[2], in Martigny, Switzerland. This demonstration room combines speech processing and computer vision algorithms to build a live 3D representation of the room, representing each visitor as an animated avatar. POM is used to provide with real-time people localization in the room using four Firewire cameras.

In the near future, our tracking system will be displayed at the Olympic Museum [3] in Lausanne, Switzerland, as part of an exhibition about Athletes and Technology.

Finally, the technology presented here might also be used as part of an industrial partnership, whose goal is to study the feasibility of using vision-based people tracking for customer market research inside shopping environments.

6.2 Future Work

Several future research directions have spawned from the work presented in this book. Among the main ones is the modification of the POM algorithm to make it more robust to non-human motion and lighting changes. POM's only input are the simultaneous images from various cameras post-processed by background subtraction. Since background subtraction detects any kind of image motion, the approach is not able to distinguish humans from other types of moving objects. Furthermore, even sophisticated background subtraction algorithms are quite sensitive to light changes in the image. In Chapter 3.3, we have demonstrated the feasibility of a multi-view

---

[1]European Commission FP6 project DYVINE `http://www.dyvine.org`

[2]Idiap Showroom `http://www.idiap.ch/the-institute/showroom`

[3]Olympic Museum, Lausanne `http://www.olympic.org/content/Olympic-Museum/`

detector working with image-based classifiers. This however came at a substantial computational cost. In its current form, our method also produced significantly more false positives than POM. Hence the interest of a new multi-view people detection algorithm that would not use - or at least not rely entirely on - background subtraction. Possible ideas include processing binary images with, for example, shape analysis, in order to remove blobs that obviously do not belong to pedestrians. The association of a classifier-based pedestrian detector with background subtraction would similarly allow to filter binary blobs from unwanted object motion. Yet another solution would be to replace the motion segmentation step altogether by another method.

Along the same lines, the use of an image-based person detector might also help in case of very crowded scenes, where people are so close to each other that the background subtraction produces a single large blob containing several people. In such cases, people are severely occluded on all camera views. Therefore, a part-based pedestrian detector, that does not look for a whole human body but searches for isolated body parts would be recommended. Calibration information could be integrated so that detectors from several camera views would combine their results in a Hough transform voting procedure.

In its current version, the POM detection algorithm solves the system of equations at its heart using a fixed point method. Despite the effectiveness of this solution and the fact that the algorithm is able to run in real-time, fixed point methods are known to be among the least efficient optimization methods. Therefore, a significant speed gain could be achieved by replacing the current optimization with a faster numerical method, such as the Newton's method.

Another potential extension of our work deals with the modification of our Linear-Programming-based tracking framework to include appearance and motion models to the optimization. Our method already produces very good results without those, but degenerate cases sometimes happen, with more than one equivalent solutions to the optimization. In these situations, several trajectories usually evolve very closely such that it is impossible to guess the correct links based on the ground plane detections alone. Those situations would benefit, for example, from an appearance model of the tracked objects. Additionally, ensuring motion consistency of the tracks might help. In the current model, a trajectory progressing in a random walk is considered as likely as a straight one. In reality, it is clear that not all movements are equally probable. Along those lines, it would be desirable to incorporate a sophisticated motion model stemming from our behavioral maps into the Linear Programming-based tracker, in a similar manner to what we did with the Dynamic Programming-based one.

The behavior model presented in Chapter 5 is a generic yet powerful method for extracting and characterizing complex motion patterns of pedestrians. This model is however not suited to any kind of statistical analysis from trajectories. For instance, analysis for sport would rather focus more on individual players and players interaction. Therefore, different types of statistical processing of people trajectories still need to be studied. This would benefit from the good quality of trajectory data our system is able to produce.

Appendix A

K-Shortest Paths Algorithm Description

In this appendix we give a short description of the K-shortest paths algorithm, used to optimize efficiently our tracking framework. The interested reader can refer to [117] for further details.

Given a directed graph $G = (V, E)$, where V is the set of vertices and E is the set of edges, the algorithm computes the k-shortest node-disjoint paths - hereafter referred only as *shortest paths* - between v_{source} and v_{sink}, iteratively for $l = 1, \ldots, k$, where k is fixed. Thus, at the lth iteration, the l-shortest paths are computed by using the $l-1$ shortest paths from the previous iteration.

Let P_l be the optimal set of l paths at iteration l. The transition from P_l to P_{l+1} is based on the idea of shortest signed paths. A *signed path* is a sequence of nodes and sign-labeled edges connecting them in order, with each edge assigned a positive label (+) if it is in the direction of the path, that is from the source to the sink, or a negative label (-) otherwise.

At iteration $l + 1$ of the algorithm, P_{l+1} can be obtained from P_l by augmenting it with a special kind of signed path p^*, called *interlacing* of P_l, which satisfies the following two conditions [117]:

1. An edge is common to both p^* and P_l if and only if it has a negative label;

2. A node is common to both p^* and P_l if and only if it is incident to an edge with negative label.

Note that the first condition is required to obtain edge-disjoint paths in P_{l+1}, which is necessary but not sufficient for node-disjoint paths. The second condition complements the first one for node-disjointness by excluding those signed paths having single node overlap with P_l.

Given a shortest edge-simple interlacing p^* of P_l, P_{l+1} can be obtained by *augmentation* of p^* and P_{l+1}, which is defined as adding positive labelled edges of p^*

147

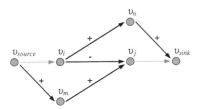

Figure A.1: An example of interlacing and the process of augmentation (only vertices that are in P_2 is shown). The shortest path are $P_1 = \{(v_{source}, v_i, v_j, v_{sink})\}$. The shortest interlacing of P_1 (bold lines with corresponding edge labels) is $p^* = (v_{source}, v_m, v_j, v_i, v_n, v_{sink})$. Augmentation of P_1 and p^* gives the optimal pair of paths $P_2 = \{(v_{source}, v_m, v_j, v_{sink}), (v_{source} v_i, v_n, v_{sink})\}$.

to P_l and removing negative labelled edges of p^* from P_l (See [117] for details). Fig. A.1 gives an example of such an augmentation, where the shortest path is

$$P_1 = \{(v_{source}, v_i, v_j, v_{sink})\}$$

and the shortest interlacing of P_1 is

$$p^* = (v_{source}, v_m, v_j, v_i, v_n, v_{sink})$$

with corresponding edges labeled respectively as $(+, +, -, +, +)$. The optimal pair of paths is obtained by augmenting P_1 and p^* as

$$P_2 = \{(v_{source}, v_m, v_j, v_{sink}), (v_{source} v_i, v_n, v_{sink})\}\,.$$

Interlacings in the original graph G correspond one-to-one to node-simple directed paths in an extended graph $G_l = (V_l, E_l)$ at iteration l of the algorithm, which can be obtained by a two-phase transformation from G, as specified in Table A.1. The first phase addresses the above-described two conditions for being an interlacing since the node-disjointness criteria is relaxed to arc-disjointness. On the other hand, the second phase represents a transformation from signed paths to directed unsigned paths. Therefore, the shortest interlacings in G are equivalent to the shortest node-simple directed paths in G_l. In addition, the cost of an interlacing in G is the same as the cost of the corresponding directed path in G_l. Fig. A.2 illustrates an example of this transformation for two nodes.

An additional edge cost transformation can be applied to G_l with possibly negative edge costs to obtain a canonic equivalent graph G_l^c with non-negative edge costs. The added benefit of this transformation is the reduction in the complexity of the shortest path computation at each iteration. Let the cost value for an edge $e_{i,j} \in E_l$ between nodes $v_i \in V_l$ and $v_j \in V_l$ be $c_{i,j}$, then G_l is transformed using the following equation [117]

$$c'_{i,j} = c_{i,j} + s_i - s_j \qquad \forall e_{i,j} \in E_l\,, \tag{A.1}$$

Table A.1: Graph Transformation Phases [117]

- Split every node v_i in P_l, except v_{source} and v_{sink} into two nodes, namely v_i' and v_i''. Assign all input, resp. output, edges of v_i to v_i', resp. v_i''. Add a directed auxiliary edge of zero cost from v_i' to v_i''.

- Reverse the direction and algebraic sign of cost for each edge in P_l, including auxiliary edges.

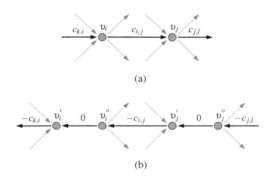

(a)

(b)

Figure A.2: The two-phase graph transformation. (a) Two nodes v_i and v_j in the original graph. Bold lines (with edge costs $c_{.,.}$) represent the arc of a shortest path incident to these two nodes. (b) The same part of the graph after the transformation.

where s_n represents the cost of the shortest path from the source node v_{source} to node v_n. In other words, at the lth iteration, G_l is cost transformed to G_l^c by using the shortest path costs of nodes in G_{l-1}^c. Note that with this transformation, cost values for all paths between the source and the sink nodes change by the same constant factor, and hence, path ordering, in terms of the cost values, remains the same.

A summary of the complete algorithm is given in Algorithm 1 in pseudo-code. The function `efficient_shortest_path` implements a shortest path algorithm that is specifically designed for non-negative edge costs. In our implementation, we used Dijkstra's single source shortest paths algorithm [29] to compute the shortest path trees at each iteration. However, since the initial graph is a DAG, the first tree is computed in linear time by using a topological sort of its vertices [25]. The total time complexity of the algorithm is $O(k(m + n \cdot \log n))$, where k is the number of objects appearing in a given time interval, m is the number of edges and n is the number of nodes in the final transformed graph.

Algorithm 1: K-Shortest Paths Algorithm for the Tracking Problem

input : a set of probabilistic occupancy maps
output: a set of k paths between v_{source} and v_{sink}
Construct the initial graph G, with edge costs from Eq. 4.38
$p_1^* \leftarrow \texttt{generic\_shortest\_path}\,(G,\, v_{source},\, v_{sink})$
$P_1 \leftarrow \{p_1^*\}$
for $l \leftarrow 1$ **to** l_{max} **do**
    if $l \neq 1$ **then**
        if $cost(P_l) \geq cost(P_{l-1})$ **then**
            return $P_{l-1} = \{p_1^*, \ldots, p_{l-1}^*\}$
        end
    end
    $G_l \leftarrow \texttt{extend\_graph}\,(\,G\,)$ /* as in Table A.1 */
    $G_l^c \leftarrow \texttt{transform\_edge\_cost}\,(G_l)$ /* according to Eq. A.1 */
    $p_{l+1}^* \leftarrow \texttt{efficient\_shortest\_path}\,(\,G_l^c,\, v_{source},\, v_{sink}\,)$
    $p^* \leftarrow \texttt{interlacing}\,(\,P_l\,)$ /* corresponding to p_{l+1}^* */
    $P_{l+1} \leftarrow P_l \cup p^*$ /* i.e., augmentation of P_l and p^* */
end

References

[1] ALEXANDRE ALAHI, YANNICK BOURSIER, LAURENT JACQUES, AND PIERRE VANDERGHEYNST. **A Sparsity Constrained Inverse Problem to Locate People in a Network of Cameras**. In *International Conference on Digital Signal Processing*, pages 1–7, July 2009. 12, 14, 33, 34, 60

[2] ERNESTO L. ANDRADE, SCOTT BLUNSDEN, AND ROBERT B. FISHER. **Modelling Crowd Scenes for Event Detection**. In *International Conference on Pattern Recognition*, **1**, pages 175–178, 2006. 3, 127

[3] NADEEM ANJUM AND ANDREA CAVALLARO. **Single Camera Calibration for Trajectory-Based Behavior Analysis**. In *IEEE Conference on Advanced Video and Signal Based Surveillance*, pages 147–152, September 2007. 3, 126

[4] GIANLUCA ANTONINI, SANTIAGO VENEGAS MARTINEZ, MICHEL BIERLAIRE, AND JEAN PHILIPPE THIRAN. **Behavioral Priors for Detection and Tracking of Pedestrians in Video Sequences**. *International Journal of Computer Vision*, **69**(2):159–180, August 2006. 127

[5] GIANLUCA ANTONINI, SANTIAGO VENEGAS, JEAN PHILIPPE THIRAN, AND MICHEL BIERLAIRE. **A Discrete Choice Pedestrian Behavior Model for Pedestrian Detection in Visual Tracking Systems**. In *Advanced Concepts for Intelligent Vision Systems*, 2004. 127

[6] KIRSTIE BALL, DAVID LYON, DAVID MURAKAMI WOOD, CLIVE NORRIS, AND CHARLES RAAB. **A Report on the Surveillance Society for the Information Commissioners office by the Surveillance Studies Network**, 2006. 1

[7] CSABA BELEZNAI, BERNHARD FRÜHSTÜCK, AND HORST BISCHOF. **Multiple Object Tracking Using Local PCA**. In *International Conference on Pattern Recognition*, pages 79–82, Washington, DC, USA, 2006. IEEE Computer Society. 81

[8] RICHARD E. BELLMAN. *Dynamic Programming*. Princeton University Press, 1957. 79, 81

[9] MAREN BENNEWITZ, WOLFRAM BURGARD, AND GRZEGORZ CIELNIAK. **Utilizing Learned Motion Patterns to Robustly Track Persons**. In *Proceedings of the Joint IEEE International Workshop on Visual Surveillance and Performance Evaluation of Tracking and Surveillance (VS-PETS)*, pages 102–109, 2003. 3, 126, 127

[10] JÉRÔME BERCLAZ, FRANÇOIS FLEURET, AND PASCAL FUA. **Robust People Tracking with Global Trajectory Optimization**. In *Conference on Computer Vision and Pattern Recognition*, **1**, pages 744–750, June 2006. 3

[11] JÉRÔME BERCLAZ, FRANÇOIS FLEURET, ENGIN TÜRETKEN, AND PASCAL FUA. **Multiple Object Tracking using Flow Linear Programming**. Technical report, EPFL — CVLab, December 2009. Submitted to *IEEE Transactions on Pattern Analysis and Machine Intelligence*. 102

[12] JÉRÔME BERCLAZ, ALI SHAHROKNI, FRANÇOIS FLEURET, JAMES FERRYMAN, AND PASCAL FUA. **Evaluation of Probabilistic Occupancy Map People Detection for Surveillance Systems**. In *IEEE International Workshop on Performance Evaluation of Tracking and Surveillance*, pages 55–62, June 2009. 46

[13] KENI BERNARDIN AND RAINER STIEFELHAGEN. **Evaluating Multiple Object Tracking Performance: The CLEAR MOT Metrics**. *EURASIP Journal on Image and Video Processing*, 2008. 22, 23

[14] JAMES BLACK, TIM ELLIS, AND PAUL ROSIN. **Multi-View Image Surveillance and Tracking**. In *IEEE Workshop on Motion and Video Computing*, pages 169–174, 2002. 3, 80

[15] LEO BREIMAN. **Bagging Predictors**. *Machine Learning*, **24**(2):123–140, 1996. 66

[16] LEO BREIMAN, JEROME FRIEDMAN, R.A. OLSHEN, AND CHARLES J. STONE. *Classification and Regression Trees*. Chapman & Hall, New York, 1984. 66

[17] GABRIEL J. BROSTOW AND ROBERTO CIPOLLA. **Unsupervised Bayesian Detection of Independent Motion in Crowds**. In *Conference on Computer Vision and Pattern Recognition*, pages 594–601, 2006. 81

[18] DUANE C. BROWN. **Close-Range Camera Calibration**. *Photogrammetric Engineering*, **37**(8):855–866, 1971. 16

[19] HUNG HAI BUI, SVETHA VENKATESH, AND GEOFF A. W. WEST. **Policy Recognition in the Abstract Hidden Markov Models**. *Journal of Artificial Intelligence Research*, **17**(1):451–499, 2002. 127

[20] QUIN CAI AND JAKE K. AGGARWAL. **Automatic Tracking of Human Motion in Indoor Scenes across Multiple Synchronized Video Streams**. In *International Conference on Computer Vision*, pages 356–362, 1998. 32

[21] SIMONE CALDERARA, RITA CUCCHIARA, AND ANDREA PRATI. **Detection of Abnormal Behaviors Using a Mixture of Von Mises Distributions**. In *IEEE Conference on Advanced Video and Signal Based Surveillance*, pages 141–146, Sept. 2007. 126

[22] ROBERT T. COLLINS. **Mean-Shift Blob Tracking through Scale Space**. In *Conference on Computer Vision and Pattern Recognition*, **02**, pages 234–240, 2003. 2, 32

[23] DORIN COMANICIU, VISVANATHAN RAMESH, AND PETER MEER. **Real-Time Tracking of Non-Rigid Objects Using Mean Shift**. In *Conference on Computer Vision and Pattern Recognition*, **2**, pages 2142–2149, 2000. 2, 3, 79

[24] DORIN COMANICIU, VISVANATHAN RAMESH, AND PETER MEER. **Kernel-Based Object Tracking**. *IEEE Transactions on Pattern Analysis and Machine Intelligence*, **25**(5):564–575, 2003. 79

[25] THOMAS H. CORMEN, CHARLES E. LEISERSON, RONALD L. RIVEST, AND CLIFFORD STEIN. *Introduction to Algorithms*. The MIT Press, 2 edition, September 2001. 149

[26] NAVNEET DALAL AND BILL TRIGGS. **Histograms of Oriented Gradients for Human Detection**. In *Conference on Computer Vision and Pattern Recognition*, **1**, pages 886–893, 2005. 32, 33

[27] GEORGE B. DANTZIG. *Linear Programming and Extensions*. Princeton University Press, Princeton, NJ, 1963. 102

[28] DAMIEN DELANNAY, NICOLAS DANHIER, AND CHRISTOPHE DE VLEESCHOUWER. **Detection and Recognition of Sports(wo)men from Multiple Views**. In *Third ACM/IEEE Interational Conference on Distributed Smart Cameras*, 2009. 33, 34

[29] EDSGER W. DIJKSTRA. **A Note on two Problems in Connexion with Graphs**. *Numerische Mathematik*, **1**:269–271, 1959. 149

[30] SHILOH L. DOCKSTADER AND A. MURAT TEKALP. **Multiple Camera Tracking of Interacting and Occluded Human Motion**. *Proceedings of the IEEE*, **89**(10):1441–1455, Oct 2001. 11

[31] WEI DU AND JUSTUS PIATER. **Multi-camera People Tracking by Collaborative Particle Filters and Principal Axis-Based Integration**. In *Asian Conference on Computer Vision*, pages 365–374, 2007. 80

[32] ALBERTO ELFES. *Occupancy Grids: A Probabilistic Framework for Robot Perception and Navigation*. PhD thesis, Carnegie Mellon University, 1989. 12

[33] AHMED ELGAMMAL, DAVID HARWOOD, AND LARRY DAVIS. **Non-parametric Model for Background Subtraction**. In *European Conference on Computer Vision*, pages 751–767, 2000. 20

[34] ANNA ELLIS, ALI SHAHROKNI, AND JAMES FERRYMAN. **Overall Evaluation of the PETS2009 Results**. In *IEEE International Workshop on Performance Evaluation of Tracking and Surveillance*, pages 117–124, June 2009. 46, 105, 116, 117

[35] MARKUS ENZWEILER AND DARIU M. GAVRILA. **Monocular Pedestrian Detection: Survey and Experiments**. *IEEE Transactions on Pattern Analysis and Machine Intelligence*, **31**(12):2179–2195, 2009. 32

[36] RAN ESHEL AND YAEL MOSES. **Homography Based Multiple Camera Detection and Tracking of People in a Dense Crowd**. In *Conference on Computer Vision and Pattern Recognition*, pages 1–8, June 2008. 3, 33, 34, 81

[37] LIXIN FAN, KAH-KAY SUNG, AND TECK-KHIM NG. **Pedestrian Registration in Static Images with Unconstrained Background**. *Pattern Recognition*, **36**(4):1019–1029, April 2003. 32

[38] MARTIN A. FISCHLER AND ROBERT C. BOLLES. **Random Sample Consensus: a Paradigm for Model Fitting with Applications to Image Analysis and Automated Cartography**. *Commun. ACM*, **24**(6):381–395, 1981. 18

[39] FRANÇOIS FLEURET, JÉRÔME BERCLAZ, RICHARD LENGAGNE, AND PASCAL FUA. **Multi-Camera People Tracking with a Probabilistic Occupancy Map**. *IEEE Transactions on Pattern Analysis and Machine Intelligence*, **30**(2):267–282, February 2008. 33, 34

[40] JEAN-SÉBASTIEN FRANCO AND EDMOND BOYER. **Fusion of Multi-View Silhouette Cues Using a Space Occupancy Grid**. In *International Conference on Computer Vision*, **2**, pages 1747–1753, 2005. 12

[41] DARIU M. GAVRILA AND STEFAN MUNDER. **Multi-cue Pedestrian Detection and Tracking from a Moving Vehicle**. *International Journal of Computer Vision*, **73**(1):41–59, June 2007. 32

[42] WEINA GE AND ROBERT T. COLLINS. **Multi-target Data Association by Tracklets with Unsupervised Parameter Estimation**. In *British Machine Vision Conference*, September 2008. 81

[43] WEINA GE AND ROBERT T. COLLINS. **Marked Point Processes for Crowd Counting**. In *Conference on Computer Vision and Pattern Recognition*, pages 2913–2920, 2009. 32

[44] JAN GIEBEL, DARIU GAVRILA, AND CHRISTOPH SCHNÖRR. **A Bayesian Framework for Multi-cue 3D Object Tracking**. In *European Conference on Computer Vision*, **4**, pages 241–252, 2004. 2, 32, 80

[45] FANNY GILLIÉRON. **Calibration Automatique d'une Caméra**. Technical report, CVLab — EPFL, 2007. 18

[46] MEI HAN, WEI XU, HAI TAO, AND YIHONG GONG. **An Algorithm for Multiple Object Trajectory Tracking**. In *Conference on Computer Vision and Pattern Recognition*, **1**, pages 864–871, June 2004. 2, 3, 32

[47] ISMAIL HARITAOGLU, DAVID HARWOOD, AND LARRY S. DAVIS. **Who, When, Where, What: A Real Time System for Detecting and Tracking People**. In *Proceedings of the Third Face and Gesture Recognition Conference*, pages 222–227, 1998. 2

[48] ISMAIL HARITAOGLU, DAVID HARWOOD, AND LARRY S. DAVIS. **W4: Real-Time Surveillance of People and Their Activities**. *IEEE Transactions on Pattern Analysis and Machine Intelligence*, 22(8):809–830, August 2000. 2, 32

[49] RICHARD HARTLEY AND ANDREW ZISSERMAN. *Multiple View Geometry in Computer Vision*. Cambridge University Press, Cambridge, UK, second edition, 2003. 16, 17

[50] DIRK HELBING. **A Fluid Dynamic Model for the Movement of Pedestrians**. *Complex Systems*, 6:391–415, 1992. 126

[51] DIRK HELBING AND PÉTER MOLNÁR. **Social Force Model for Pedestrian Dynamics**. *Phys. Rev. E*, 51(5):4282–4286, May 1995. 126

[52] WEIMING HU, MIN HU, XUE ZHOU, TIENIU TAN, JIANGUANG LOU, AND STEVE MAYBANK. **Principal Axis-Based Correspondence between Multiple Cameras for People Tracking**. *IEEE Transactions on Pattern Analysis and Machine Intelligence*, 28(4):663–671, 2006. 34

[53] WEIMING HU, XUEJUAN XIAO, ZHOUYU FU, DAN XIE, TIENIU TAN, AND STEVE MAYBANK. **A System for Learning Statistical Motion Patterns**. *IEEE Transactions on Pattern Analysis and Machine Intelligence*, 28(9):1450–1464, 2006. 126

[54] CHANG HUANG, BO WU, AND RAMAKANT NEVATIA. **Robust Object Tracking by Hierarchical Association of Detection Responses**. In *European Conference on Computer Vision*, pages 788–801. Springer-Verlag, 2008. 81

[55] IBM. **ILOG CPLEX**. http://www.ilog.com/products/cplex/. 102

[56] MICHAEL ISARD AND ANDREW BLAKE. **CONDENSATION-Conditional Density Propagation for Visual Tracking**. *International Journal of Computer Vision*, 29(1):5–28, August 1998. 32

[57] MICHAEL ISARD AND JOHN MACCORMICK. **BraMBLe: a Bayesian Multiple-Blob Tracker**. In *International Conference on Computer Vision*, **2**, pages 34–41, July 2001. 3, 14, 32

[58] SACHIKO IWASE AND HIDEO SAITO. **Parallel Tracking of all Soccer Players by Integrating Detected Positions in Multiple View Images**. In *International Conference on Pattern Recognition*, **4**, pages 751–754, August 2004. 80

[59] HAO JIANG, SIDNEY FELS, AND JAMES J. LITTLE. **A Linear Programming Approach for Multiple Object Tracking**. In *Conference on Computer Vision and Pattern Recognition*, pages 744–750, 2007. 3, 82

[60] NEIL JOHNSON AND DAVID HOGG. **Learning the Distribution of Object Trajectories for Event Recognition**. *Image and Vision Computing*, 14(8):609 – 615, 1996. 6th British Machine Vision Conference. 3, 126

[61] JINMAN KANG, ISAAC COHEN, AND GÉRARD G. MEDIONI. **Tracking People in Crowded Scenes across Multiple Cameras**. In *Asian Conference on Computer Vision*, 2004. 3, 79, 89

[62] NARENDRA KARMARKAR. **A New Polynomial Time Algorithm for Linear Programming**. *Combinatorica*, 4(4):373–395, 1984. 102

[63] RANGACHAR KASTURI, DMITRY GOLDGOF, PADMANABHAN SOUNDARARAJAN, VASANT MANOHAR, JOHN GAROFOLO, MATTHEW BOONSTRA, VALENTINA KORZHOVA, AND JING ZHANG. **Framework for Performance Evaluation of Face, Text, and Vehicle Detection and Tracking in Video: Data, Metrics, and Protocol**. *IEEE Transactions on Pattern Analysis and Machine Intelligence*, 31(2):319–336, February 2009. 22, 117

[64] SAAD M. KHAN AND MUBARAK SHAH. **A Multiview Approach to Tracking People in Crowded Scenes Using a Planar Homography Constraint**. In *European Conference on Computer Vision*, **4**, pages 133–146, 2006. 3, 33, 34, 63, 68

[65] SAAD M. KHAN AND MUBARAK SHAH. **Tracking Multiple Occluding People by Localizing on Multiple Scene Planes**. *IEEE Transactions on Pattern Analysis and Machine Intelligence*, 31(3):505–519, 2009. 3, 33, 34, 81

[66] SOHAIB KHAN, OMAR JAVED, AND MUBARAK SHAH. **Tracking in Uncalibrated Cameras with Overlapping Field of View**. In *2nd IEEE Workshop on Performance Evaluation of Tracking and Surveillance*, 2001. 32

[67] ZIA KHAN, TUCKER BALCH, AND FRANK DELLAERT. **MCMC-Based Particle Filtering for Tracking a Variable Number of Interacting Targets**. *IEEE Transactions on Pattern Analysis and Machine Intelligence*, 27(11):1805–1918, 2005. 80

[68] KYUNGNAM KIM AND LARRY S. DAVIS. **Multicamera Tracking and Segmentation of Occluded People on Ground Plane Using Search-Guided Particle Filtering**. In *European Conference on Computer Vision*, pages 98–109, 2006. 3, 33, 34

[69] FRANCISCO KLAUSER. **'Lost' French CCTV-Studies**. *Surveillance & Society*, 6(1), 2009. 1

[70] NILS KRAHNSTOEVER AND PAULO R. S. MENDONÇA. **Bayesian Autocalibration for Surveillance**. In *International Conference on Computer Vision*, 2, pages 1858–1865, October 2005. 18

[71] JOHN KRUMM, STEVE HARRIS, BRIAN MEYERS, BARRY BRUMITT, MICHAEL HALE, AND STEVE SHAFER. **Multi-Camera Multi-Person Tracking for EasyLiving**. *Visual Surveillance, IEEE Workshop on*, pages 3–10, 2000. 33

[72] SOLOMON KULLBACK AND RICHARD LEIBLER. **On Information and Sufficiency**. *The Annals of Mathematical Statistics*, 22(1):79–86, March 1951. 35, 38

[73] ALESSANDRO LANZA, LUIGI DI STEFANO, JÉRÔME BERCLAZ, FRANÇOIS FLEURET, AND PASCAL FUA. **Robust Multi-View Change Detection**. In *British Machine Vision Conference*, Warwick, UK, September 2007. 20

[74] BASTIAN LEIBE, KONRAD SCHINDLER, AND LUC J. VAN GOOL. **Coupled Detection and Trajectory Estimation for Multi-Object Tracking**. In *International Conference on Computer Vision*, pages 1–8, Oct. 2007. 81

[75] BASTIAN LEIBE, EDGAR SEEMANN, AND BERNT SCHIELE. **Pedestrian Detection in Crowded Scenes**. In *Conference on Computer Vision and Pattern Recognition*, 1, pages 878–885, San Diego, CA, June 2005. 32

[76] YUAN LI, CHANG HUANG, AND RAMAKANT NEVATIA. **Learning to Associate: Hybrid-Boosted Multi-Target Tracker for Crowded Scene**. In *Conference on Computer Vision and Pattern Recognition*, pages 2953–2960, June 2009. 3, 81

[77] DEREK R. MAGEE. **Tracking Multiple Vehicles Using Foreground, Background and Motion Models**. *Image and Vision Computing*, 22(2):143–155, February 2004. 80

[78] EMILIO MAGGIO, MURTAZA TAJ, AND ANDREA CAVALLARO. **Efficient multi-target visual tracking using Random Finite Sets**. *IEEE Transactions On Circuits And Systems For Video Technology*, 18(8):1016–1027, August 2008. 80

[79] A. MAKHORIN. **GLPK- GNU Linear Programming Kit**, 2008. http://www.gnu.org/software/glpk/. 102, 121, 122

[80] DIMITRIOS MAKRIS AND TIM ELLIS. **Learning Semantic Scene Models from Observing Activity in Visual Surveillance**. *IEEE Transactions on Systems, Man, and Cybernetics, Part B*, 35(3):397–408, June 2005. 126, 127

[81] MATHWORKS. **MATLAB**. http://www.mathworks.com/. 102

[82] THOMAS MAUTHNER, MICHAEL DONOSER, AND HORST BISCHOF. **Robust Tracking of Spatial Related Components**. In *International Conference on Pattern Recognition*, pages 1–4, 2008. 80

[83] STEPHEN J. MAYBANK AND OLIVIER D. FAUGERAS. **A Theory of Self-Calibration of a Moving Camera**. *International Journal of Computer Vision*, 8(2):123–151, 1992. 16

[84] MICHAEL MCCAHILL AND CLIVE NORRIS. **CCTV in London**. UrbanEye, Working Paper No. 6, June 2002. 1, 125

[85] IVANA MIKIC, SIMONE SANTINI, AND RAMESH JAIN. **Video Processing and Integration from Multiple Cameras**. In *Proceedings of the 1998 Image Understanding Workshop*, San Francisco, 1998. 3

[86] ANURAG MITTAL AND LARRY S. DAVIS. **M2Tracker: A Multi-View Approach to Segmenting and Tracking People in a Cluttered Scene Using Region-Based Stereo**. In *European Conference on Computer Vision*, pages 18–33, 2002. 33

[87] ANURAG MITTAL AND LARRY S. DAVIS. **M2Tracker: A Multi-View Approach to Segmenting and Tracking People in a Cluttered Scene**. *International Journal of Computer Vision*, 51(3):189–203, 2003. 33, 34, 63, 80, 89

[88] ANURAG MITTAL AND LARRY S. DAVIS. **A General Method for Sensor Planning in Multi-Sensor Systems: Extension to Random Occlusion**. *International Journal of Computer Vision*, 76(1):31–52, January 2008. 10

[89] VLAD I. MORARIU AND OCTAVIA I. CAMPS. **Modeling Correspondences for Multi-Camera Tracking Using Nonlinear Manifold Learning and Target Dynamics**. In *Conference on Computer Vision and Pattern Recognition*, **1**, pages 545–552, 2006. 34

[90] ANDREW NAFTEL AND SHEHZAD KHALID. **Classifying Spatiotemporal Object Trajectories Using Unsupervised Learning in the Coefficient Feature Space**. *Multimedia Systems*, **12**(3):227–238, December 2006. 3, 126

[91] CHIKAHITO NAKAJIMA, MASSIMILIANO PONTIL, BERND HEISELE, AND TOMASO POGGIO. **Full-body person recognition system**. *Pattern Recognition*, **36**(9):1997–2006, September 2003. 33

[92] PETER NILLIUS, JOSEPHINE SULLIVAN, AND STEFAN CARLSSON. **Multi-target tracking - Linking identities using Bayesian network inference**. In *Conference on Computer Vision and Pattern Recognition*, **2**, pages 2187–2194, 2006. 81

[93] CLIVE NORRIS AND MICHAEL MCCAHILL. **CCTV: Beyond Penal Modernism?** *British Journal of Criminology*, **46**(1):97–118, 2006. 125

[94] KENJI OKUMA, ALI TALEGHANI, NANDO DE FREITAS, JAMES J. LITTLE, AND DAVID G. LOWE. **A Boosted Particle Filter: Multitarget Detection and Tracking**. In *European Conference on Computer Vision*, pages 28–39, Prague, Czech Republic, May 2004. 2, 80

[95] NURIA OLIVER, BARBARA ROSARIO, AND ALEX PENTLAND. **A Bayesian Computer Vision System for Modeling Human Interactions**. *IEEE Transactions on Pattern Analysis and Machine Intelligence*, **22**(8):831–843, August 2000. 20, 21

[96] KAZUHIRO OTSUKA AND NAOKI MUKAWA. **Multi-View Occlusion Analysis for Tracking Densely Populated Objects Based on 2-D Visual Angles**. In *Conference on Computer Vision and Pattern Recognition*, **1**, pages 90–97, 2004. 3, 14, 33

[97] SANGHO PARK AND MOHAN M. TRIVEDI. **Multiperspective Video Analysis of Persons and Vehicles for Enhanced Situational Awareness**. *Intelligence and Security Informatics*, **3975**:440–451, 2006. 34

[98] LUIS PATINO, HAMID BENHADDA, ETIENNE CORVÉE, FRANÇOIS BRÉMOND, AND MONIQUE THONNAT. **Extraction of Activity Patterns on Large Video Recordings**. *Computer Vision, IET*, **2**(2):108–128, June 2008. 3, 126

[99] A. G. AMITHA PERERA, CHUKKA SRINIVAS, ANTHONY HOOGS, GLEN BROOKSBY, AND WENSHENG HU. **Multi-Object Tracking Through Simultaneous Long Occlusions and Split-Merge Conditions**. In *Conference on Computer Vision and Pattern Recognition*, **1**, pages 666–673, June 2006. 81

[100] MASSIMO PICCARDI. **Background Subtraction Techniques: a Review**. In *IEEE International Conference on Systems, Man and Cybernetics*, **4**, pages 3099–3104, October 2004. 19

[101] CLAUDIO PICIARELLI, GIAN LUCA FORESTI, AND LAURO SNIDARO. **Trajectory Clustering and its Applications for Video Surveillance**. In *IEEE Conference on Advanced Video and Signal Based Surveillance*, pages 40–45, September 2005. 3, 126

[102] JULIEN PILET, CHRISTOPH STRECHA, AND PASCAL FUA. **Making Background Subtraction Robust to Sudden Illumination Changes**. In *European Conference on Computer Vision*, **4**, pages 567–580, Marseille, France, October 2008. 20, 21

[103] MARC POLLEFEYS, REINHARD KOCH, AND LUC VAN GOOL. **Self-Calibration and Metric Reconstruction Inspite of Varying and Unknown Intrinsic Camera Parameters**. *International Journal of Computer Vision*, **32**(1):7–25, 1999. 16

[104] JONATHAN D. RYMEL, JOHN-PAUL RENNO, DARREL GREENHILL, JAMES ORWELL, AND GRAEME A. JONES. **Adaptive Eigen-Backgrounds for Object Detection**. In *International Conference on Image Processing*, **3**, pages 1847–1850, October 2004. 20

[105] KOICHI SATO AND JAKE K. AGGARWAL. **Temporal Spatio-Velocity Transform and its Application to Tracking and Interaction**. *Computer Vision and Image Understanding*, **96**(2):100–128, November 2004. 79

[106] ANDREAS SCHADSCHNEIDER. **Cellular Automaton Approach to Pedestrian Dynamics - Theory**. *Pedestrian and Evacuation Dynamics*, pages 75 – 86, 2002. 126

[107] BERNT SCHIELE AND JAMES L. CROWLEY. **A Comparison of Position Estimation Techniques Using Occupancy Grids**. *Robotics and Autonomous Systems*, **12**(3):163–169, 1993. 12

[108] ARMIN SEYFRIED, BERNHARD STEFFEN, WOLFRAM KLINGSCH, AND MAIK BOLTES. **The Fundamental Diagram of Pedestrian Movement Revisited**. *Journal of Statistical Mechanics: Theory and Experiment*, **2005**(10), 2005. 126

[109] KHURRAM SHAFIQUE AND MUBARAK SHAH. **A Noniterative Greedy Algorithm for Multiframe Point Correspondence**. *IEEE Transactions on Pattern Analysis and Machine Intelligence*, **27**(1):51–65, January 2005. 81, 82

[110] HIROAKI SHIMIZU AND TOMASO POGGIO. **Direction Estimation of Pedestrian from Multiple Still Images**. In *IEEE Intelligent Vehicles Symposium*, pages 596–600, 2004. 33

[111] KEVIN SMITH, DANIEL GATICA-PEREZ, AND JEAN-MARC ODOBEZ. **Using Particles to Track Varying Numbers of Interacting People**. In *Conference on Computer Vision and Pattern Recognition*, 1, pages 962–969, 2005. 2, 3, 80

[112] CHRIS STAUFFER AND W. ERIC L. GRIMSON. **Adaptive Background Mixture Models for Real-Time Tracking**. In *Conference on Computer Vision and Pattern Recognition*, 2, pages 246–252, 1999. 20

[113] CHRIS STAUFFER AND W. ERIC L. GRIMSON. **Learning Patterns of Activity Using Real-Time Tracking**. *IEEE Transactions on Pattern Analysis and Machine Intelligence*, 22(8):747–757, August 2000. 3, 126, 127

[114] PETR STEPAN, MIROSLAV KULICH, AND LIBOR PREUCIL. **Robust Data Fusion With Occupancy Grid**. *Systems, Man, and Cybernetics, Part C: Applications and Reviews, IEEE Transactions on*, 35(1):106–115, February 2005. 12

[115] RAINER STIEFELHAGEN, KENI BERNARDIN, RACHEL BOWERS, JOHN S. GAROFOLO, DJAMEL MOSTEFA, AND PADMANABHAN SOUNDARARAJAN. **The CLEAR 2006 Evaluation**. In *Multimodal Technologies for Perception of Humans*, pages 1–44, 2006. 21, 22, 46, 47

[116] PATRICK P. A. STORMS AND FRITS C. R. SPIEKSMA. **An LP-based Algorithm for the Data Association Problem in Multitarget Tracking**. *Computers & Operations Research*, 30(7):1067–1085, June 2003. 82

[117] J. W. SUURBALLE. **Disjoint Paths in a Network**. *Networks*, 4:125–145, 1974. 8, 79, 97, 103, 147, 148, 149

[118] MÁTÉ SZARVAS, AKIRA YOSHIZAWA, MUNE-TAKA YAMAMOTO, AND JUN OGATA. **Pedestrian Detection with Convolutional Neural Networks**. In *Intelligent Vehicles Symposium*, pages 224–229, June 2005. 33

[119] HAI TAO, HARPREET S. SAWHNEY, AND RAKESH KUMAR. **Object Tracking with Bayesian Estimation of Dynamic Layer Representations**. *IEEE Transactions on Pattern Analysis and Machine Intelligence*, 24(1):75–89, 2002. 79

[120] DAVID THIRDE, MARK BORG, JAMES FERRYMAN, FLORENT FUSIER, VALÉRY VALENTIN, FRANÇOIS BRÉMOND, AND MONIQUE THONNAT. **A Real-Time Scene Understanding System for Airport Apron Monitoring**. In *Proceedings of the Fourth IEEE International Conference on Computer Vision Systems*, pages 26–33, 2006. 11

[121] SEBASTIAN THRUN. **Learning Occupancy Grid Maps with Forward Sensor Models**. *Autonomous Robots*, 15(2):111–127, 2003. 12

[122] ERIC TÖPFER, LEON HEMPEL, AND HEATHER CAMERON. **Islands and Networks of Visual Surveillance in Berlin**. UrbanEye, Working Paper No. 8, December 2003. 1

[123] BILL TRIGGS. **Autocalibration and the Absolute Quadric**. In *Conference on Computer Vision and Pattern Recognition*, pages 609–614, 1997. 16

[124] ROGER Y. TSAI. **A Versatile Camera Calibration Technique for High-Accuracy 3D Machine Vision Metrology Using Off-the-Shelf TV Cameras and Lenses**. *IEEE Journal of Robotics and Automation*, 3(4):323–344, August 1987. 16, 17, 18

[125] JACO VERMAAK, ARNAUD DOUCET, AND PATRICK PÉREZ. **Maintaining Multi-Modality through Mixture Tracking**. In *International Conference on Computer Vision*, 2, pages 1110–1116, October 2003. 80

[126] PAUL A. VIOLA AND MICHAEL J. JONES. **Rapid Object Detection using a Boosted Cascade of Simple Features**. In *Conference on Computer Vision and Pattern Recognition*, 1, pages 511–518, 2001. 14, 43, 66

[127] PAUL A. VIOLA, MICHAEL J. JONES, AND DANIEL SNOW. **Detecting Pedestrians using Patterns of Motion and Appearance**. In *International Conference on Computer Vision*, pages 734–741, 2003. 32, 33

[128] C. WILLIAM WEBSTER. **CCTV Policy in the UK: Reconsidering the Evidence Base**. *Surveillance & Society*, 6(1), 2009. 2

[129] CARSTEN WIECEK AND ANN RUDINOW SAETNAN. **Restrictive? Permissive? The Contradictory Framing of Video Surveillance in Norway and Denmark**. UrbanEye, Working Paper No. 4, March 2002. 1

[130] JACK K. WOLF, AUDREY M. VITERBI, AND GLENN S. DIXON. **Finding the Best Set of K Paths through a Trellis with Application to Multitarget Tracking**. *Aerospace and Electronic Systems, IEEE Transactions on*, 25(2):287–296, Mars 1989. 81

[131] BO WU AND RAMAKANT NEVATIA. **Tracking of Multiple, Partially Occluded Humans based on Static Body Part Detection**. In *Conference on Computer Vision and Pattern Recognition*, 1, pages 951–958, June 2006. 79

[132] BO WU AND RAMAKANT NEVATIA. **Detection and Tracking of Multiple, Partially Occluded Humans by Bayesian Combination of Edgelet based Part Detectors**. *International Journal of Computer Vision*, **75**(2):247–266, November 2007. 32, 33

[133] GANG WU, YI WU, LONG JIAO, YUAN-FANG WANG, AND EDWARD Y. CHANG. **Multi-Camera Spatio-Temporal Fusion and Biased Sequence-Data Learning for Security Surveillance**. In *ACM Multimedia*, pages 528–538, 2003. 11

[134] MING XU, JAMES ORWELL, AND GRAEME A. JONES. **Tracking Football Players with Multiple Cameras**. In *International Conference on Image Processing*, **5**, pages 2909–2912, October 2004. 80

[135] CHANGJIANG YANG, RAMANI DURAISWAMI, AND LARRY DAVIS. **Fast Multiple Object Tracking via a Hierarchical Particle Filter**. In *International Conference on Computer Vision*, pages 212–219, 2005. 80

[136] DANNY B. YANG, HÉCTOR H. GONZÁLEZ-BAÑOS, AND LEONIDAS J. GUIBAS. **Counting People in Crowds with a Real-Time Network of Simple Image Sensors**. In *International Conference on Computer Vision*, pages 122–129, 2003. 3, 33, 35

[137] ALPER YILMAZ, OMAR JAVED, AND MUBARAK SHAH. **Object Tracking: A Survey**. *ACM Comput. Surv.*, **38**(4):13, 2006. 80

[138] QIAN YU, GÉRARD MEDIONI, AND ISAAC CO-HEN. **Multiple Target Tracking Using Spatio-Temporal Markov Chain Monte Carlo Data Association**. In *Conference on Computer Vision and Pattern Recognition*, pages 1–8, June 2007. 80

[139] BEIBEI ZHAN, PAOLO REMAGNINO, AND SER-GIO A. VELASTIN. **Mining Paths of Complex Crowd Scenes**. *Advances in Visual Computing*, **3804**:126–133, 2005. 127

[140] LI ZHANG, YUAN LI, AND RAMAKANT NEVA-TIA. **Global Data Association for Multi-Object Tracking Using Network Flows**. In *Conference on Computer Vision and Pattern Recognition*, 2008. 3, 82

[141] LI ZHANG, BO WU, AND RAMAKANT NEVA-TIA. **Detection and Tracking of Multiple Humans with Extensive Pose Articulation**. In *International Conference on Computer Vision*, October 2007. 33

[142] ZHENGYOU ZHANG. **A Flexible New Technique for Camera Calibration**. *IEEE Transactions on Pattern Analysis and Machine Intelligence*, **22**(11):1330–1334, November 2000. 16

[143] TAO ZHAO AND RAMAKANT NEVATIA. **Tracking Multiple Humans in Complex Situations**. *IEEE Transactions on Pattern Analysis and Machine Intelligence*, **26**(9):1208–1221, September 2004. 14, 32

[144] TAO ZHAO AND RAMAKANT NEVATIA. **Tracking Multiple Humans in Crowded Environment**. In *Conference on Computer Vision and Pattern Recognition*, **2**, pages 406–413, 2004. 2

[145] QIANG ZHU, MEI-CHEN YEH, KWANG-TING CHENG, AND SHAI AVIDAN. **Fast Human Detection Using a Cascade of Histograms of Oriented Gradients**. In *Conference on Computer Vision and Pattern Recognition*, **2**, pages 1491–1498, 2006. 32, 33

CPSIA information can be obtained
at www.ICGtesting.com
Printed in the USA
LVHW042118191222
735540LV00003B/521